Signposts to Freedom

Signposts to Freedom

Jan Milič Lochman

THE TEN COMMANDMENTS AND CHRISTIAN ETHICS

Translated from the German by *David Lewis*

AUGSBURG Publishing House • Minneapolis

82070211

Translation Copyright © 1982 Ausburg Publishing House and
Christian Journals Limited.

Library of Congress Catalog Card No. 81-052283

International Standard Book No. 0-8066-1915-5

Scripture quotations unless otherwise noted are from the
Revised Standard Version of the Bible, copyright 1946, 1952,
and 1971 by the Division of Christian Education of the
National Council of Churches.

This book is a translation of *Wegweisung der Freiheit: Abriss
der Ethik in der Perspektive des Dekalogs,* © Gütersloher
Verlagshaus Gerd Mohn, Gütersloh 1979.

Manufactured in the United States of America

Contents

Preface   9

The Ten Commandments according to Exodus 20:1-17   11

**Introduction: The Decalogue as a Guide for Christian
    Ethics?**   13
A disputed approach   13
Beyond legalism and licence   16

The Preamble: The Name of God   21
The sign outside the bracket   21
The inauguration of freedom   22
Ethics as the free response of gratitude   28

The First Commandment: to God alone the Glory   33
The first and greatest commandment   33
Freedom in danger   34
Idolatry as debasement of the currency   39
Soli Deo gloria   42

**The Second and Third Commandments: From Image to Divine
    Name**   45
An Israelite peculiarity?   45
Safeguard against the encroachments of image-making   47
How does God become concrete?   51
Against the misuse of God's name   52

The Fourth Commandment: The Festival of Freedom   57
Disciplinary measure or invitation to freedom?   57
The two versions of the Fourth Commandment   60
The ethics of Sunday   63
The ethos of anxiety, industriousness, and success   67

The Fifth Commandment: Authority and Reverence for Life   73
No leap over the wall!   73
An easy commandment?   74
Freedom as God's creatures   76
'Honour' – not 'worship'!   79
The increase of life   83
The imperative in the norms   85

The Sixth Commandment: You Shall Not Kill   87
The Archimedean point of ethics?   87
A commandment with many facets   88
Borderline cases of killing:
   (1) Suicide   94
   (2) Abortion   97
War as a borderline case?   101

The Seventh Commandment: You Shall Not Commit Adultery   105
The debris of church history   105
The man-woman relationship: the basic form of co-humanity   107
The shared life of marriage   111
Freedom from the tyrannies of lovelessness   115

The Eighth Commandment: You Shall Not Steal   119
Focus on kidnapping   119
Pressures in the direction of slavery   122
Theft 'from above' and theft 'from below'   125
The Janus face of property   128

The Ninth Commandment: Truth for the Neighbour   133
Witnessing to the truth   133
Life as a judicial process   135
Advocacy in favour of the neighbour and of grace   139
What is meant by 'telling the truth'?   142

The Tenth Commandment: You Shall Not Covet   147
Difficulties of interpretation   147
The sidelong glance   149
Who is my neighbour?   155
An eccentric ethic   159

Notes   161
Index of Names   165
Index of Biblical References   166

The English version of the Bible generally used in this work is the *Revised Standard Version*. Existing English translations of other works cited have been used where available, sometimes slightly altered for the sake of clarity in context. Dr Lochman kindly read the translation in manuscript and his suggestions were taken into this final version.

Centuries ago, Dr Dod, an eminent Cambridge Puritan, earned the affectionate nickname of 'Decalogue Dod' for his very popular *Plaine and Familiar Exposition of the Ten Commandments*. Whether the plainness of Dr Lochman's original has survived sufficiently in translation will be for the reader to judge. 'Familiar' (in the current sense of the term) it is not, neither in the original nor in English dress. For it presents one of the most ancient and central of biblical texts in an astonishingly unfamiliar modern light. The Decalogue acquires here a freshness, power and immediacy which many have believed irretrievably lost.

At least one reader in the English-speaking world is grateful to Dr Lochman for his achievement and wishes to take this opportunity of expressing the hope that many others will read it and do so with the same exhilaration and profit. All who teach the faith and all who seek faith and understanding will find treasure here. So, you see, for one reader, the author is already 'Decalogue Lochman'! Why not!

Geneva, October 1980   *David Lewis*

Preface

The first impression the Ten Commandments ever made on me was a purely visual one. On one of the otherwise bare walls of the living room of my grandparents' farm in East Bohemia there was a vivid painting of the Decalogue. As a little lad not yet going to school, I often gazed at that picture. Even when I was older I could hardly make out the words, written as they were in the old Gothic script, but I knew they were the two tables of Moses: four commandments of the left and six on the right. Soon I had to get them by heart, including some archaic Czech words which I did not really understand.

What a dismal childhood memory, you may say. How awful to have been exposed to the strict laws of Moses from early infancy! But in fact, the atmosphere of my Calvinist parents' and grandparents' home introduced me to an experience of a very different kind. It was an atmosphere of real down-to-earth delight – in the good gifts of creation, the solidarity of the human family, neighbours and church, and also, as the most natural thing in the world, in the good commandments of God. This may explain why, later on, as a theologian, I found it difficult to understand how people in the Church today and in the past could adopt theological positions which give the Decalogue a wide berth and contrast the joyful Gospel with the 'gloomy Law'. Right from infancy I had learned to see the Ten Commandments themselves, and not just the 'glad tidings' of the New Testament, as a liberating message as the 'other form of the Gospel'. The 119th Psalm which we so often sang in our prayer meetings and church services is one long sustained hymn of praise to God for His gift of the Law. We have not been left simply to fend for ourselves in the ordering of our lives. Whether our attempts to do so are successful or not, the guidance afforded by the Ten Commandments, far from hindering and enslaving, in fact encourages and liberates us. The Ten Commandments are 'signposts to freedom'.

As I learned later, this view of the Ten Commandments is one which is deeply rooted in the thinking of the Czech

Reformers, in the Hussite struggle to establish the binding and liberating force of God's Law, and also in the thought and action of the Czech Brethren with its emphasis on the 'sweet discipline' of a life shaped and directed by fellowship with God. But this view is to be found not only in our church tradition but also in the philosophical tradition of thinkers like Thomas G. Masaryk and Emanuel Radl, who considerably influenced the direction of my own thought. As they wrestled to discover the meaning of human life, both individual and social, their deepest concern was with 'freedom under the law'. It was no accident that one of the last recorded utterances of my philosophy teacher and friend, Jan Patocka, clearly pointed in this same direction, in the eminently contemporary context of the struggle for human rights: 'However well-equipped technologically, no human society can exist without a moral basis, a conviction which is more than mere opportunism, pragmatism and calculated self-interest.'

The ensuing sketch of an ethic illuminated by the Ten Commandments owes much to this bias in the tradition which has shaped my thought and action. I realize that this bias is challenged by many people in the Church and in society generally. We shall have to examine its biblical and theological basis. It will have to be tested in the fire of contemporary ethical challenges. The following pages are no more than a few steps in this direction. I invite my readers to advance the enquiry by pursuing their own researches.

Jan Milič Lochman

Basle
14th September 1978

TEN COMMANDMENTS ACCORDING TO EXODUS 20:1-17

And God spoke all these words, saying: 'I AM THE LORD YOUR GOD, WHO BROUGHT YOU OUT OF THE LAND OF EGYPT, OUT OF THE HOUSE OF BONDAGE.

YOU SHALL HAVE NO OTHER GODS BEFORE ME.

YOU SHALL NOT MAKE FOR YOURSELF A GRAVEN IMAGE, OR ANY LIKENESS OF ANYTHING THAT IS IN HEAVEN ABOVE, OR THAT IS IN THE EARTH BENEATH, OR THAT IS IN THE WATER UNDER THE EARTH; YOU SHALL NOT BOW DOWN TO THEM OR SERVE THEM; FOR I THE LORD YOUR GOD AM A JEALOUS GOD, VISITING THE INIQUITY OF THE FATHERS UPON THE CHILDREN TO THE THIRD AND THE FOURTH GENERATION OF THOSE WHO HATE ME, BUT SHOWING STEADFAST LOVE TO THOUSANDS OF THOSE WHO LOVE ME AND KEEP MY COMMANDMENTS.

YOU SHALL NOT TAKE THE NAME OF THE LORD YOUR GOD IN VAIN; FOR THE LORD WILL NOT HOLD HIM GUILTLESS WHO TAKES HIS NAME IN VAIN.

REMEMBER THE SABBATH DAY, TO KEEP IT HOLY. SIX DAYS YOU SHALL LABOUR, AND DO ALL YOUR WORK; BUT THE SEVENTH DAY IS A SABBATH TO THE LORD YOUR GOD; IN IT YOU SHALL NOT DO ANY WORK, YOU, OR YOUR SON, OR YOUR DAUGHTER, YOUR MANSERVANT, OR YOUR MAIDSERVANT, OR THE SOJOURNER WHO IS WITHIN YOUR GATES; FOR IN SIX DAYS THE LORD MADE HEAVEN AND EARTH, THE SEA AND ALL THAT IS IN THEM, AND RESTED THE SEVENTH DAY; THEREFORE THE LORD BLESSED THE SABBATH AND HALLOWED IT.

HONOUR YOUR FATHER AND YOUR MOTHER, THAT YOUR DAYS MAY BE LONG IN THE LAND WHICH THE LORD YOUR GOD GIVES YOU.

YOU SHALL NOT KILL.

YOU SHALL NOT COMMIT ADULTERY.

YOU SHALL NOT STEAL.

YOU SHALL NOT BEAR FALSE WITNESS AGAINST YOUR NEIGHBOUR.

YOU SHALL NOT COVET YOUR NEIGHBOUR'S HOUSE; YOU SHALL NOT COVET YOUR NEIGHBOUR'S WIFE, OR HIS MANSERVANT, OR HIS MAIDSERVANT, OR HIS OX, OR ANYTHING THAT IS YOUR NEIGHBOUR'S.

The Decalogue as a Guide for Christian Ethics?

A Disputed Approach

Anyone seeking to develop an outline of Christian ethics today on the basis of the Ten Commandments must be quite clear as to the controversial character of such an undertaking. It can be challenged not only by pointing out how vital it is for an ethic to speak to the contemporary world but also on fundamental theological grounds.

1. In view of the contemporary intellectual and cultural situation, in view of the way our contemporaries think and act, the way we *ourselves* think and act, surely the intellectual world of the Decalogue has become utterly alien to us? Between our present age and these commandments, is there not a great gulf fixed, 'a nasty big ditch' (Lessing)? This is certainly the case from a *historical* standpoint. The Decalogue is a very ancient biblical text; in respect of its antecedents, it is undoubtedly one of the oldest texts not only of the biblical but even of the pre-biblical tradition. It emerged in social and cultural conditions which defy comparison with those prevailing today. The very first sentence makes this clear: it speaks of slavery in Egypt. In other words, it has reference to the conditions of a society of slaves. But, for us, this is a pattern of society which has long been a thing of the past. What ethical guidance can we possibly derive for our conduct of life today, in the era of late capitalism and socialism, from a text originating in almost pre-historic times? If we take our bearings from the Decalogue, surely we are condemned in advance to find ourselves in a cul-de-sac? If we take the Ten Commandments as our starting point, how can we possibly speak effectively to the condition of our contemporaries and to our own needs and concerns?

2. The same scepticism is in place when we consider the *conditions* in which we live today. The Decalogue has become

foreign to us not merely from a theoretical standpoint but also in practice, in respect of the way life is actually lived today. There has been a dramatic change in our cultural pattern. Gerhard Ebeling draws attention to this in his book on the Ten Commandments: 'For centuries the Ten Commandments provided the basic pattern of life for those peoples who accepted the authority of the biblical tradition. The Decalogue was the basic moral framework of our western civilization; every child learned it by heart as the standard of personal conduct. But today the Ten Commandments have largely lost their authority.'[1] Even earlier, of course, these commandments were largely ignored and skilfully evaded in the 'Christian' world, but only *per nefas* and with a bad conscience. Today, however, the validity and good sense of the Ten Commandments are radically challenged by many currents of thought and from many standpoints and the struggle for 'emancipation' from them is waged with a good conscience.

Ebeling gives examples of this typically modern attitude. The attack is directed not just against the commandments of the *First* Table, i.e., life lived in the presence of God, although there are many who regard this First Table as 'outmoded' and 'continuing a shadowy existence only in what can be lumped together under the heading of "superstition"'. The attack is also, even chiefly, directed against the Second Table, for this 'directly affects our social conditions'. 'The reaction here, therefore, is more emotionally charged. The command to honour father and mother is even regarded as symptomatic of an authoritarian and repressive social order from which we need to be emancipated. Moreover, the prohibition of adultery and all its implications in the ordering of family life and sexual attitudes seems a rather feeble barrier which is no longer capable of containing the floodwaters of sexuality',[2] Nor is the situation essentially different in respect of the prohibition of killing. The validity of this prohibition is certainly plainer than ever today and in certain contexts its imperative force has even been strengthened. We think, for example, of the challenge to the 'normality' of the death penalty and of war. On the other hand, the increase in brutality and violence today makes it hard to deny that this commandment, too, is in many ways losing its force and often even being suspended altogether. We are becoming increasingly insensitive to mass slaughter and death.

This picture of conditions in our world may be one-sided. Yet Ebeling is surely right to point out the changes taking place in our habitual moral assumptions at so many levels, changes which make the Ten Commandments appear out-moded even from the standpoint of the way people actually live today. In view of all this, therefore, does it still make sense to continue using the Decalogue as a basis for our discussion of Christian ethics?

3. The same question can also be raised from the standpoint of *Christian theology*. The Decalogue is an Old Testament text. Certainly a central and classic Old Testament text but nevertheless a *pre-Christian* text. The Christian ethic, in the full sense of the term, is surely one which springs only from the ethos of the New Testament as a whole. When Jesus declared: 'But I say to you . . .' was he not pointing out *new* patterns of conduct to an audience whose ethical thinking was controlled precisely by these Ten Commandments? It may be said that he was giving a new edge and sharpness to the old commandments; but did he not, at the same time, take them up into, and so 'abolish' them in, the dynamic and liberating movement of love? Nothing was more alien to Jesus than a legalistic view of the Law. Surely, however, legalism is the constant danger of an ethic of the Ten Commandments? If we take our ethical bearings from the Decalogue, do we not run the risk of jettisoning this provocative and stimulating new element in the ethics of the New Testament (as understood, moreover, by the apostle Paul himself)? Surely the position we should adopt is that of Luther who boldly affirmed: 'If we have Christ, it will be easy for us to make laws and judge all things rightly. Indeed we will even make new decalogues, as Paul did in all his letters, and Peter, too, and first and foremost, Christ himself in the Gospel. And these decalogues are clearer than that of Moses, as Christ's face is clearer than that of Moses.'[3] This may invite misunderstanding but in the last analysis it is evangelically sound.

Attracted to this solution, many simply reject the Decalogue as a guide for Christian ethics and instruction. For example, in a Basle dissertation, 'Kirche am Sinai' (1965), H. Röthlisberger examines in detail the centuries-old and almost

universal educational practice of the churches, the Reformed
Churches in particular, and comes to the conclusion that the
Decalogue seems to make it 'almost impossible for catechists to
breathe the atmosphere of the New Testament. When they are
taught the Ten Commandments, Christians suddenly find
themselves members of the people of Israel, fearful, trembling
and standing afar off' (p.113). In short, an ethic based on the
Decalogue is surely a hopeless historical and theological retreat
which leads us into a cul-de-sac in Christian theology and in
Christian education.

Both questions deserve consideration. They cannot be
brushed under the carpet. They point to real problems and
dangers. There are in fact traditional and contemporary mis-
conceptions and difficulties associated with an ethic based on
the Decalogue, and they affect not only the possibilities of
winning the intellectual assent of our contemporaries but also
our chances of effectively communicating distinctive Christian
positions. If we are to explore such an ethic responsibly, we
must consider these questions, therefore, and try to clear them
up as far as possible. Nor must we lose sight of these problems
when we seek to interpret the individual commandments. But
before we come to them, let me here offer, in a provisional way
and in an initial approach, my reasons for believing, despite
weighty objections, that even today there can be a promising
and fruitful approach to Christian ethics via the Decalogue. I
take each set of questions in turn.

Beyond Legalism and Licence

Both sets of arguments presuppose a definite prior-
understanding of the Decalogue. The Ten Commandments are
seen as timeless universal laws which seek to contain human
life within a 'system' of general regulations. They therefore
represent a moralistic and legalistic view of human life and the
world. On such a view, the Decalogue is undeniably a fatal
burden on a truly Christian ethic, and this in the two directions
indicated above. If laws are interpreted *legalistically,* they
shackle ethics to the conditions which prevailed at the time of
their promulgation. They become backward looking and fail to
speak to the condition of our contemporaries in their (and our)

own very different social context and stage of cultural development. Specifically, the 'ox' and 'ass' of the Decalogue, which clearly and vividly indicate its period of origin, i.e. in a very early stage of human history in an agrarian and nomadic society, no longer concern us in any comparable way today. Most of us associate these animals with holidays or the zoo, but not with our familiar everyday life. This illustrates the general problem. On a legalistic interpretation, the reference of the Decalogue to the actual world in which we live is fatally impaired by the changed circumstances of our present life and its historical remoteness from the world in which the Decalogue originated.

The same is also true from a theological standpoint. If the Ten Commandments are interpreted legalistically and moralistically, they lapse back into 'pre-Christian' conditions and views. They are literally *pre*-Christian in the sense that they return to the time prior to the 'ethical revolution' of Jesus. Christ's condemnation of all entrenched moralism and legalism, which is certainly characteristic of the 'ethic of Jesus', applies also to a legalistic interpretation of the Decalogue. A 'Christian' education and ethic based on a legalistic interpretation of the Ten Commandments do indeed represent aberrant developments of the kind condemned by Röthlisberger and others. Christian ethics is then infiltrated by a new legalism which, from the New Testament standpoint, is a 'sin against the Holy Spirit', the kind of lapse implicit in the attitude of the Galatians who submitted again to the 'yoke' of bondage to the law and were called very sharply to order by the apostle Paul for that very reason. This legalistic way makes it much more difficult for us to have access not only to our contemporaries but also, and above all, to the very heart of the Gospel itself.

Here in particular it must be made quite clear that to interpret the Ten Commandments legalistically and moralistically is to misunderstand them not just from the standpoint of the New Testament but also from that of the original context of the Decalogue itself. Recent Old Testament scholarship rightly points out that to regard the Decalogue as a timeless universal code of moral rules is to misunderstand it completely. Certainly the 'Ten Words' preserve vital insights of immemorial human tradition. But when they emerge in the specific setting of the

Old Testament and in the concrete liturgical practice of Israel, they take on a new significance, at once more dynamic and more concrete. Gerhard von Rad points out in his *Theology of the Old Testament* that 'Israel understood and celebrated the revelation of the divine commands as a saving event of the first order'.[4] This saving event was the establishment of the covenant at Sinai within the framework of the Exodus, an event which was truly fundamental and constitutive for Israel, the people of God. In respect of its origin and its role in the faith and life of Israel and of the Christian Church, therefore, the Decalogue is the *Magna Carta* of the Covenant, the title deeds of the history of Israel's liberation.

I wish to emphasize here three elements in this definition of the Decalogue: history, covenant, and liberation.

1. The Decalogue is seen in the Old Testament as part of the salvation history and also, therefore, as a witness to *historical events*. The revelation of the Ten Commandments comes to Israel, the people of God, not from somewhere beyond space and time but very concretely, at a particular time and in a particular place: i.e. at Sinai during the events of the Exodus. The text of the Decalogue is quite inseparable from this actual history and can never be understood correctly in isolation from that history. To interpret the Decalogue legalistically is to tear it out of this living context and so to sterilize it. To make the Decalogue the basis of an abstract universal non-historical ethic is completely to ignore the origin and nature of the commandments.

2. Specifically, the historical anchorage of the Decalogue implies its character as the *title deeds of the Covenant*. Von Rad is surely right: 'The intimate connection between commands and covenant must be kept in view in all circumstances.' This was certainly how the Decalogue was understood in Israel: the two tables of the Ten Commandments were deposited in the Ark of the Covenant. They also had a central role in the liturgy of God's people. The Decalogue played a vital part in the celebration of one of Israel's most significant festivals, the renewal of the covenant at Shechem every seven years (Deut.31:10f.). This is of importance in understanding the commandments. 'With this celebration Israel gave expression to the fact that the event of revelation at Sinai remained

equally relevant for all times; it was renewed through each succeeding generation; it was contemporary for them all (cf.Deut.5:2-4; 29:10ff.).'[6] We are to look for the real significance of the commandments in the context of the covenant. To look back to them is always to look forward; it is a summons to keep the covenant at every new present moment and with a view to the future. From the biblical standpoint, therefore, the covenant is not a completed event receding further and further into the past but an eschatological event, one which is therefore open-ended and pregnant with the future.

3. The real purpose and goal of this covenant event, and of the Decalogue, too, therefore, also follows clearly from its anchorage in history. This covenant event is the Exodus, i.e. the *history of liberation* of the people of God, that all-important sequence of events on which this people's very existence rested. The divine covenant with Israel established Israel's freedom and set the seal on it. The celebration of the renewal of this covenant was a constantly renewed festival of freedom, the renewal of this freedom. Within this quite specific context Israel was given the Ten Commandments through Moses. The purpose of 'teaching' the Decalogue in the people of the Old Covenant and the New, every seven years at the festival of the renewal of the covenant but also in ordinary daily life, was to maintain and exercise this God-given freedom. This document of the covenant, essentially, is a *charter of freedom*. The Ten Commandments are the 'Ten Great Freedoms'. Only within this decisive setting of the history of Israel's deliverance can their original significance be understood. They have very little to do with legalism and moralism and a great deal to do with the struggle to understand 'the freedom of a Christian'.

Certainly there is a *vital* connection between the commandments and this struggle to understand Christian freedom. They enable us to see the practical meaning of this gift of freedom. They provide the people of God with a compass and with signposts to enable it to find the way to freedom. They bar the way not only to a legalistic misunderstanding of freedom but also to an antinomian misunderstanding of freedom, i.e. to a liberal or libertarian (mis)understanding of freedom. And ethics is rightly concerned with this danger, too. There can be no question of suspending or abandoning the Decalogue as a fundamental guide for Christian ethics simply on the grounds that it has so often been so grievously misunderstood in the practice of the Church through the centuries. I find it impossible to endorse trends in this direction, as represented by Röthlisberger's book, for example, however praiseworthy they may be in other respects. It is not only not necessary to abandon the Ten Commandments to the legalists and moralists, it would also be a mistake. It makes more sense to try to understand their original purpose and aim, both theologically and in practice. The concern for freedom is certainly not out of date but remains indeed a burning issue for all human beings, in our times especially. In the history of liberation, the battlefronts may shift but the basic concern remains the same.

The root concern for freedom takes the contemporary form of a *struggle on two fronts*. I remind you here of the change in approach to the Decalogue diagnosed earlier with the aid of Gerhard Ebeling. *First,* against legalistic and moralistic currents, which are particularly strong in our own churches, not least the Reformed, but not only in the churches. There is also a considerable degree of legalism and moralism even in the secular world, both East and West, especially among the traditionalists and conservatives. *Secondly,* a struggle against antinomian and amoralistic currents in the contemporary ethos, against the liberalism and libertarianism of those who have made a fetish of 'emancipation'.

If there can be no question of abandoning the Ten Commandments to the legalistics, neither can we leave the concern for freedom, written as it is into the very texture and fabric of the Decalogue, to the libertarians. Genuine human freedom is not just a blank cheque for us to fill out as we please. Precisely here, in this creative dialectic of the history of freedom documented and disclosed in the Bible, I find the permanent and positive human significance of the Ten Commandments. The attempt to provide an introduction to a Christian ethic based on the Ten Commandments has seemed to me a timely undertaking in face of the contemporary ethos and a promising and fruitful one in view of the biblical heritage which guides our thought and action.

THE PREAMBLE:
The Name of God

The Sign outside the Bracket

'*I am the Lord your God, who brought you out of the land of Egypt, out of the house of bondage' (Ex.20:2)*. Nowhere is the character of the Decalogue as the Magna Carta of biblical freedom more clearly expressed than here in this opening sentence, the preamble to the Ten Commandments. In most traditional expositions this introductory sentence is neglected. It is treated merely as the necessary scaffolding or framework for the really important contents, i.e. the commandments. In my view, however, something very much more important is conveyed in these introductory words. Our understanding of the whole Decalogue and all its details directly depends on correctly understanding this preamble. If we go astray here, if we miss this entrance, we are committing ourselves from the very beginning to a direction where our understanding of the individual commandments is also imperilled or even made quite impossible. Concretely, our treatment of this *pro*logue will determine whether our understanding of the Decalogue is 'evangelical' or 'legalistic and moralistic'. This preamble is a 'sign outside the bracket' which affects everything within the bracket. Everything depends on whether this sign is positive or negative.

What exactly is this 'sign before the bracket'? It is the *pre*-sentation, the *intro*-duction of the name of God. The essential thing is the linking of the divine name with the historical event of the Exodus, the linking of God with the history of salvation and the deliverance of God's people from Egyptian bondage. The Decalogue opens with this signature: '*I am Yahweh your God*'. And this name is at once defined: '*who brought you out of the land of Egypt, out of the house of bondage'*. By linking God with liberation, the freedom of this people with God, the preamble floodlights the source, the foundation and, at the same time, the overriding intention of the Decalogue, the Alpha and the Omega of God's commandments and indeed, of any ethics claiming to be biblical and Christian. In what follows we shall examine these basic aspects of the opening sentence of the Decalogue in more detail.

The Inauguration of Freedom

To many people today it is obvious that a resounding historical deliverance could provide the basis for and open up the way to a genuine human ethic. This is, in fact, the basic principle of Marxist social theory and ethics. It is in revolutionary action and in the ultimate victory of revolution that advances and initiatives take place which lead in the direction of a worthier and really responsible human life. Yet it is all the more vehemently denied here that such advances and initiatives could possibly have anything whatever to do with God. The young Marx asserted categorically: 'A *being* sees himself as independent only when he stands on his own feet, and he only stands on his own feet when he owes his *existence* to himself. A man who lives by the grace of another regards himself as a dependent being. But I live completely by the grace of another if I owe him not only the maintenance of my life but also its *creation*, if he is the *source* of my life. My life is necessarily grounded outside itself if it is not my own creation.'[7]

What Marx means by this 'other' being who robs humanity of its dependence is, of course, the biblical God, the Creator and Redeemer. The logical corollary of this identification is that human freedom requires the abolition of this God. As long as I believe in him I am not standing on my own two feet, not truly emancipated, and therefore not 'truly' human. There is undeniably a certain force and validity in this criticism, in Marx's insistence that there is a fundamental opposition between the question of liberation and the question of God. How frequently in church history, not to mention the history of religion in general, has the concept of God been developed in a decidedly despotic form and religious faith or superstition used consistently to counter human aspirations for freedom! Indeed, this almost seems to have been the rule rather than the exception in the approach of the Church and its theologians. Considering what has actually happened in the history of doctrine and the Church, Marx's criticism is not all that wide of the mark. Yet this criticism must be repudiated if it claims, as it does, that its target is the biblical message, the biblical concept of God and of faith in him, and that this criticism does justice to i.e. demolishes, this target. In fact, this criticism is guilty of overlooking something essential in its haste.

For in the biblical understanding of God and faith the position is quite different. Far from despising, still less rejecting the liberation of humankind, of our 'essential humanity', so rightly stressed by Marx, and, inseparable from this, the radical protest against everything which disables and enslaves us, the biblical message actually establishes and confirms this liberation and this protest more than ever before. The Bible proclaims this liberation and this protest as the cause where human history and the divine history of salvation coincide, as the ultimate purpose of the covenant, as not only the core of the biblical promise (the Gospel) but also the direction in which the commandments (the Law) point us; in other words, as an unconditional and not just a contingent concern. Certainly this is the direction in which the preamble to the Decalogue, to the first and great commandment, points us: 'I am Yahweh your God, who brought you out of the land of Egypt, out of the house of bondage'. From its standpoint, God and liberation are inseparably united.

Are we indulging here in mere postulates and pious assumptions? To my mind, something far more substantial is involved. Take for example the historical event of the Exodus as attested in the Old Testament. The historical details of this event may elude us but we are dealing here with a real exploit, a real breakthrough, and also a real basis for a continuous succession of new initiatives in Israel's history. Or consider the resurrection of Christ, the New Testament parallel to the Exodus. From the very beginning, the resurrection of Jesus was seen as a new and universal Exodus, the final identification of God with the cause of human liberation, an Exodus which in the Christian mission is not only proclaimed but also put into practice by the Christian witnesses. This incomparable departure 'into all the world' was a many-sided 'campaign for freedom' which changed the course of history. Think, too, of all the comparable efforts in the history of the Church. Even if these efforts were perhaps the exception rather than the rule, they nevertheless repeatedly rediscovered the original and authentic 'rule' of the biblical tradition and tried to put it into practice. We may add that many Marxists today are keenly aware of the strength of the biblical faith, this unique 'feature' of the name of God. 'With Zeus, Jupiter, Marduk, Ptah or even with the bogeyman, Thomas Münzer could not possibly have achieved the change he actually inaugurated by his appeal to the Exodus from Egypt and to the far from meek and mild Jesus of Nazareth.'[8] An atheist has a keener eye here for the real significance of the divine name in the Bible (and in the Decalogue!) than many church goers and theologians, namely, the inauguration of the history of freedom – God's *and* humanity's!

What is the significance of this inauguration of freedom, this perspective of the first commandment, for human life, for our *condition humaine*? What difference does it make for us to be reminded of the divine name in this perspective? Let me suggest three essential elements, three *liberation programmes,* disclosed and discernible along with this link between God and freedom established in the Bible. They may be labelled: the demythologizing of nature, the defatalizing of history, and the dethronement of death.

(a) There is a very close connection between the biblical name of God and the predicate '*Creator*'. Also, incidentally, in the direction of the Exodus event. Some Old Testament scholars consider the Old Testament faith in creation to have been the fruit of the Exodus. The earliest witnesses connect liberation from the land of Egypt with faith in Yahweh's act of creation. Faith in the Creator means that humanity is no merely cosmic being. We are, of course, that too. We belong to the created world, depend on its natural processes, are part of that world. But it is impossible to reduce humanity to these natural processes, these dependent relationships and interconnections with nature, without remainder. Conditioned by nature we are also God's creatures. There is a dimension to our life which can never be exhaustively defined or understood in purely natural terms. We are 'two-dimensional' beings: we exist in a relationship ('in the covenant') which transcends the 'horizontal' conditions of our life and which makes our life an unconditioned, unique, irreplaceable existence, however conditioned it may be biologically, physiologically and cosmologically. This also means, however, that we are not to regard, accept or worship nature, the actual conditions of our earthly existence, as if they were the absolutely determinative factors. By this faith in creation, we break through the idea of nature as 'divine', of the cosmic forces as absolute. The world is world and not God. It can and should be 'demythologized', i.e. seen, handled and mastered as creation, no more and no less. It is no accident that the human 'dominium' (and at the same time our 'ministerium') is established right from the start in the first biblical account of creation (Gen.1:28). With the biblical name of God, therefore, a critical distance from nature and a mandate to control and shape it are secured for humanity, and in this way an essential dimension of our human freedom.

(b) According to the preamble to the Decalogue, the biblical name of God is connected even more directly with *history.* I have already pointed out more than once – understandably in view of the central place in takes in the preamble – that the deliverance from Egypt was an historical event. God 'introduces himself' in this historical act of liberation. The significance of this for our human life in history is that we are not the helpless slaves of history nor its mere 'playthings'. We are conditioned by history, of course, inextricably entangled in the fabric of historical events and relationships. Our life does not begin *ab ovo;* we are inserted in a predetermined historical situation, that of our particular nation, class, church, family. For many aspects of our life, therefore, the direction is already set. The forces of history exercise control over us. And in our personal and social destiny, there are, to be sure, real blind alleys and 'houses of bondage' awaiting us. It is little wonder that so many thoughtful people view history with a certain despair, denying that there is any meaning in history and still more, that there is any connection between God and history.

But the Bible does not despair of history – and the Preamble to the Decalogue is an eloquent testimony to this. The biblical witnesses take their cue from the experience of the Exodus and use this experience to interpret our human situation in face of

the cul-de-sacs of history. God has taken up our human cause,
especially that of the hopelessly enslaved. In this name, therefore, i.e. because of Yahweh your God who brought Israel out
of Egypt, out of the house of bondage (because also, it must be
added here in New Testament language, of the God who
identified himself with us completely in the history of Jesus of
Nazareth, in the Easter history of Christ), no 'house of
bondage' is ever again irrevocable, there are no longer any
final 'blind alleys', there is no ultimate 'fate'. Biblical faith in
God 'disarms' the 'power of (blind) fate': it defatalizes human
history, including above all, my personal 'lot' in history.

(c) The linking of the divine name with the history of
freedom also changes our situation in another final and decisive way, namely, in respect of the *problem of death*. Death is
the most serious riposte to any history of liberation. Every
dream of freedom, every commitment to freedom, finally
comes to an end here. Death is the complete and absolute
'counter-Utopia', the full-stop, the final point in every sense,
but supremely and pointedly in the direction of freedom.
Nowhere is our own impotence and the power of the 'other' so
painfully clear as here, in the face of death. If there is such a
thing as a 'house of bondage', it is surely this 'house of death'.

The Bible is supremely realistic in tackling this question too,
displaying not a trace of religious romanticism. The Old Testament's bitterest complaints are reserved for this threat to
human existence, especially to meaningful human existence
before God. 'Who can give thee praise in Sheol (the realm of
death)?', asks the psalmist (Ps.6:5) with utter frankness. The
apostle is equally frank: 'Wretched man that I am! Who will
deliver me from this body of death?' (Rom.7:24). There is no
toning-down of the harshness of this servitude in the Bible.
Biblical humanity – including Jesus himself – is not eased of
this burden of death by any idea of immortality of the kind so
often and so eloquently advanced in the history of religion and
philosophy. There is no 'natural' immortality in the Bible, no
immortality *'etsi Deus non daretur'* (even if God did not exist).

What we do find in the Bible, however, is the message of
God's presence, indeed, his faithfulness in the situation of
death. This, too, is an element in the 'introduction of the divine
name' in the Decalogue in response to the human question

about true freedom. The Egyptian 'house of bondage' refers directly, of course, to the actual historical enslavement of the people of Israel in Egypt. But it is no accident that this 'house of bondage' should have been so soon singled out as symbolic of the final eschatological slavery and peril of death's dominion, as a symbol of the chaos menacing God's good creation. Shyly and undogmatically, yet quite unmistakably, the Exodus already provides a promise in face of Sheol, even in the Old Testament. If God supports humanity's longing for freedom, it is permissable for us to hope that the history of liberation inaugurated with the Exodus will not come to a halt at the threshold of death.

This hope is fulfilled in a central and unambiguous way in the Easter history of Jesus: the resurrection is confirmation of the divine and human freedom in the situation of death. *Exodus patet* – there is a way out. Even this final 'house of bondage' must render up its victims. The same apostle who groaned, 'Wretched man that I am!' and asked 'Who will deliver me from this body of death?' (and this was no mere rhetorical question) declares in the very next breath: 'Thanks be to God through our Lord Jesus Christ!' (Rom.7:24f.). And the ground on which Paul justified this 'leap' of faith was not the supposed indestructibility of the human soul nor the powers of nature or of history, but, clearly and unambiguously, an appeal to the liberating God of the Exodus and to his faithfulness as demonstrated in the Old Testament and in the New.

Paul's words in the eight chapter of Romans (Rom.8:38f.) seem to me to point in the same direction and may now be quoted as a summary of the previous points: 'For I am sure that neither life nor death, nor angels nor principalities, nor things present, nor things to come, nor powers, nor height nor depth, nor anything else in all creation will be able to separate us from the love of God in Christ Jesus our Lord.' I regard these words as the New Testament pendant to the introduction of the divine name in the Decalogue. There are no other gods beside this God. Even death itself, the ultimate power on earth, is dethroned. Certainly the freedom established in this divine name is and will continue to be threatened and assailed in life and in death by the onslaught of the rebel powers, and compromised by constant failure due to our own laziness or presumption. This freedom is never in our 'possession', therefore, as something we can count on and control automatically or arbitrarily, or worse still, self-righteously. We are never more than pilgrims, beginners, in the history of freedom. But because this freedom is rooted in and maintained by the Old and New Covenant of the God 'who brought you out of the land of Egypt, out of the house of bondage', it does not, despite all our lapses, remain merely an idle dream, the last desperate throw of the headstrong gambler. In the one abiding name there are sufficient funds to cover this venture of freedom. In life and in death, therefore, freedom remains our promise.

Ethics as the free Response of Gratitude

In these reflections on the 'preamble' to the Decalogue, we have offered just a few hints about the background and purpose of the Ten Commandments. They could be developed and we shall have an opportunity to do this when we turn to the individual commandments. But from what has already been said it will be clear, I hope, that this introductory sentence of the Decalogue is no mere flourish which could be ignored in the more detailed study ahead. The 'signature', the 'sign outside the bracket', affects everything inside the bracket. It indicates the direction for the whole of the Decalogue and for each of its individual components, and also, in a broader and more inclusive sense, for the whole field of *theological ethics*. I end this chapter with three explanatory comments on this last point.

1. Theological ethics is no arbitrary, independent and self-contained discipline. In the light of the preamble to the first commandment, it can only be properly understood as *response, discipleship, obedience*. Ethics is the response of faith, an attempt to draw the consequences, the determination to act accordingly, indeed, discipleship (imitation, following after) in the sense in which Dietrich Bonhoeffer rightly recommended evangelical theology to regard it. This was how Jesus himself understood his own 'ethics' – as a summons to discipleship. This was also how it is required in the New Testament letters, both in *substance* (recollecting the teaching and example of Jesus) and in *principle,* with methodological implications, since

the imperative, the apostolic 'law' of these letters, follows from the indicative, the apostolic Gospel. The standpoint of the Decalogue is thus adopted and carried further in the New Testament by being clarified and filled out in the light of christology.

Because of this inseparable connection between the Christian ethic and the history of salvation, because of this introduction of the divine name and work before all other names and works, the Christian ethic can never be regarded as an *ethic of works and achievement*. This is the special temptation precisely of those thinkers who rightly stress the importance of ethics. They tend to regard ethical conduct not simply as right conduct but also as conduct which justifies and saves. The way to salvation is a practical one, via good works or revolutionary civil action. Think of some outstanding names in the modern period, of Kant and Marx, for example; but also of the old movements of Jewish piety at the time of Jesus, or of Christian pietism at the time of the Reformation. All these names and movements have considerable achievements to their credit. They were exemplary in their obedience to commandments – including those of the Decalogue. But they ignored one vital aspect of the biblical ethic: they turned the ethical way into an absolute and so tended to become legalistic or moralistic, attaching overmuch emphasis to performance and achievement. In classical theological terminology, they tended to advocate a 'works righteousness'. In so doing, they obscured the prevenience of grace and tended therefore to become the exponents of a 'loveless' self-righteous morality.

Christian ethics must be clearly distinguished from all such tendencies. It does not spring from and flourish on the soil of the success and glory of our own human deeds. It is the active response to a liberation revealed to and conferred on Christians. Good action is what corresponds to this liberation, what mirrors salvation but does not bring salvation. This is why grace, – grace from God but also grace towards our fellow human beings – continues to be the distinctive feature and decisive dimension of this ethic. Above all, this is also why moralism and legalism, because of their tendency to relative 'lovelessness', so often 'native' even in Christian circles, are so dangerous and damaging for evangelical ethics.

2. If ethics is understood as a response, the next question is what sort of response. At this stage we are not concerned to define this response in detail but simply to identify its basic texture and direction, and the word I wish to mention first and to emphasize in this context is the word 'gratitude'. This term, as you may know, plays an important part in the *Heidelberg Catechism,* which deals with the Decalogue in its third and concluding section. The two preceding sections are headed 'Of Human Need' and 'Of Human Redemption' respectively. The third section, the 'ethical' part of the Catechism, is entitled 'Of Gratitude'. This distribution of the material undoubtedly does justice to a basic element in the thrust of the Decalogue which we have tried to identify in the light of the preamble to the Ten Commandments. The appropriate response to the historical deliverance inaugurated for us in the name of Yahweh and in the name of Jesus Christ, the matching directive for discipleship, is the response of thankfulness. The primary effect of faith is the gratitude, the knowledge and confession of the people of God that it owes its freedom and its hope to God.

But the human attitude suggested by such terms as 'gratitude', 'indebtedness', 'thankfulness' is one which is open to misunderstanding and challenged, even downright unpopular nowadays. We need only recall the statement quoted earlier from Karl Marx, where he says that human beings are not really free, not really human, so long as they are still 'indebted' to another. And it is true that there are forms of indebtedness which are enslaving and disabling. Above all, a 'gratitude' which is imposed on us, expected of us and accompanied by sanctions is an extremely questionable thing, indeed, actually counterproductive as a spur to ethical action. I remember from my youth a certain beggar who preferred to call on non-church people in their homes rather than on known churchgoers. The reason he gave was that when he received alms from the non-church goers at least he wasn't expected to show his gratitude by pretending to be pious! That should make us pause. Our contemporaries have quite respectable reasons for their suspicion of the word 'gratitude', (The same is also true in quite secular contexts. Almost the surest way of making people heartily sick of 'spontaneous' ethical and political enthusiasm in socialist countries is for moralistic politicians to be constantly telling them to show their gratitude for some particular Party accomplishment by enthusiastically performing some corresponding effort in return!)

Despite all possible misuse, however, it is hardly to be denied that spontaneous gratitude is potentially a creative force which can release ethical energies. Think for example of the Old Testament and the gratitude for the divine law in Psalm 119. The instruction contained in the law is not a 'demand' but a 'permission', an authorization to be obedient, the praxis of 'indebtedness' an ethic of grace. The same is true of the ethics of the New Testament. Think of the New Testament letters, not only their exhortations but also their characteristic pattern, with the apostolic instructions following after the praise of God's grace and as an attestation of the gift of freedom. This confers on them the character of a promise of and an encouragement and invitation to a reasonable, spontaneous, 'charismatic' behaviour and activity. Nothing could be further removed from its spirit than the deadliness of a legalistic and moralistic approach.

3. This aspect of the biblical ethic is very clearly expressed in the words of the apostle Paul: 'For freedom has Christ set us free; stand fast, therefore, and do not submit again to a yoke of slavery' (Gal.5:1). These words were uttered in the heat of one of the sharpest conflicts the apostle ever had to engage in within and on behalf of his churches, namely, his struggle with the legalists who wanted to lead the 'liberated people' back into the 'house of bondage' of a legalistic 'works righteousness'. But Paul's exhortation has an abiding significance, embodying as it does the fundamental presupposition of any Christian ethic, namely, that Christ has set us free for freedom. I regard this statement as the New Testament equivalent of the preamble to the Decalogue. Prior to all Christian thought and action stands this preamble which proclaims the *liberation which has been bestowed,* the Exodus from the house of bondage, the opening of the door to the freedom graciously promised and accomplished by God. The Gospel precedes the Law. What decides whether an ethic is Christian or not, i.e. whether or not it takes its direction from the Bible, is its respect for and obedience to this 'sequence' (Gospel and Law), which Karl Barth in particular has commended to evangelical theology in recent years.

It must also be emphasised, however, that the 'Law' *follows* the Gospel; indeed, that the Law is – in Barth's phrase – the 'other form' of the Gospel. 'Ethics as response' (P. Lehmann), 'advocacy of the Spirit' (H. van Oyen), cannot take any other form than this persistence in and demonstration of the freedom for which Christ has set us free. In Old Testament language, it can only consist in keeping and illustrating the covenant established in the Exodus history of freedom. But this persistence in and demonstration of freedom is a way with 'definite', 'distinctive' binding features. The freedom for which Christ has set us free is no vague and empty freedom but a freedom which displays the same characteristics as Jesus Christ himself. Or again, in Old Testament terms, it is a way which has been officially signposted in the commandments of the Decalogue. To follow these indications, to be directed by these signposts, is in the interests of our true freedom. Christian ethics is anchored in the concrete liberation granted us in the salvation history: it is practised and developed as a freedom under obligation.

THE FIRST COMMANDMENT:
To God alone the Glory

The first and greatest commandment

'*You shall have no other gods before me!*' Throughout the history of the Church it has been emphasised that this commandment is the 'first' not just because it stands at the beginning but because these words are the most important in the Decalogue. It is also 'the greatest' because it introduces, establishes and governs all the rest. Luther, for example, underlines the supreme importance of the First Commandment by summarising it in a memorable paraphrase in his *Small Catechism*: 'We should fear, love and trust in God above all things' and by adopting the formal device of echoing this paraphrase throughout his exposition of the other Commandments when introducing each with the words: 'We should fear and love God . . .'[9] In this way Luther stresses that all the other Commandments are governed by the First, together with its Preamble. They follow from it, clarifying its fundamental directive and applying it concretely to various areas and relationships of our human life.

This is wholly in accord with the biblical view of the Ten Commandments. We can even appeal to Jesus himself here. Asked which is the 'great commandment', he replies: 'You shall love the Lord your God with all your heart and with all your soul and with all your mind. This is the great and first commandment' (Mt.22:37f.). Jesus' words summarize the 'First Table' of the Decalogue, just as his next words summarize the 'Second Table': 'You shall love your neighbour as yourself!' Jesus' summary of the First Table clearly reproduces the intention of the First Commandment: 'You shall have no other gods before me!'

This First Commandment is intimately connected with and

indeed inconceivable without the Preamble and, for the most part, has been rightly regarded as the First Commandment only in conjunction with it. From this 'great and first' commandment onwards, therefore, the imperative ('you shall') is clearly inseparable from the indicative ('I am . . .'). The signposts presuppose the new way opened up by the deliverance from bondage. The converse is also true, however. The indicative passes over into the imperatives which signpost the newly opened way. The liberation experienced by Israel is to be translated into the practice of freedom. In New Testament terms: 'For freedom did Christ set us free' and we are to 'stand fast', therefore, and not get 'entangled again in a yoke of bondage' (Gal.5:1). This is the inherent logic and at the same time the goal established in the command: 'You shall have no other gods before me!'

Freedom in danger

The command is tailored to a human situation in which freedom is in danger. The hallmark of the biblical understanding of freedom is its recognition of this danger. This is what differentiates it from all optimistic liberal views of freedom. The ideology of progress and freedom which has been so influential in modern times assumed that, if human spontaneity were given its head by the removal of contingent historical obstacles, an ultimately irresistible process of liberation would automatically be set in train. The best guarantee of progress in freedom and freedom in progress, it was thought, was a policy of laissez-faire, laissez-passer, of non-interference and permissiveness. This approach became the received wisdom in the dominant mental climate of the 19th century, for example, in the still influential 'liberal economics' and can still be found today in the field of 'progressive' sexual morality and educational theory. On the assumptions underlying this way of thinking, the 'command to be free' is really a contradiction in terms. Freedom is spontaneity and spontaneity is freedom.

The biblical view of freedom is more realistic. Not that it sets little store by freedom. Biblical anthropology has even less in common with theoretical and pragmatic pessimists who propose radically authoritarian structures as protection against possible abuses of freedom than it has with enlightened liberals with their laissez-faire policies. It is for the very opposite reason that the Bible is more realistic. Just because it sets so much store by freedom, it is all the more keenly aware of the dangers to which freedom is constantly exposed. To 'stand fast' in freedom is no sinecure. The way of freedom is a narrow way, not easy to find, for it follows a narrow line between temptations from both within and without. We can fall *out* of freedom, find it troublesome and complicated and begin to cast around for old familiar long established systems and 'legal guarantees' (just as the New Testament Galatians did, much to Paul's dismay). But we can also come a cropper *in* freedom by abusing it, by making it 'an occasion to the flesh' (i.e. by selfish licence) instead of an opportunity to love (as Paul warned those other Galatians whose temptation lay in the opposite direction – Gal.5:13). Between these two temptations to legalism and licence, between 'nomianism' and 'anti-nomianism', as they have been called, lies the narrow way of genuine freedom, the freedom to which we are invited in the covenant, in Christ.

This is the context, the frame or reference, of the First Commandment. What precisely does the command, 'You shall have no other gods before me!' mean? Is it the solemn assertion of a monotheistic principle which is then to be made an obligatory article of faith? Right down to recent times scholars have believed that the existence of such a monotheistic creed at so early a stage was due to Moses himself.[10] But this can hardly be true historically. 'A Yahweh cult existed for a long period in Israel which was undoubtedly interpreted officially in the sense of the First Commandment but was not monotheistic. We speak, therefore, of henotheism or monolatry' (G.von Rad).[11] But even from a theological standpoint, the monotheistic hypothesis does not square with the real intention of the First Commandment. The latter is not concerned to maintain a general principle or to lay down a rational theological principle. Something very concrete and dynamic is required here; namely the keeping of the covenant, the demonstration of fidelity in the midst of very real temptations: the clear-cut out-and-out rejection of the extremely real danger and seductiveness of 'other gods'. Of course, a monotheistic position did indeed develop in the Old Testament from this exclusive

devotion to Yahweh specifically required by this First Commandment. But the latter is concerned not with monotheism as
such but with Israel's 'standing fast' in the covenant, its believing, thinking and action on the basis of the Exodus.

The truth of this is documented by the events at Sinai as
reported in the book of Exodus. This describes a tremendous
crisis in which the freedom just acquired by the people of God
is put to the test. The people of God fails this test. Hardly has it
tasted freedom than it begins to doubt whether this freedom is
really worthwhile. It soon seems to them in retrospect that
there was a good deal to be said in favour of the land of Egypt,
the house of bondage. When freedom turns out to entail risks
and make demands, they hanker increasingly for the 'fleshpots
of Egypt'. Tensions develop again and again between a small
minority which is prepared to 'stand fast in freedom' despite all
temptations, and the large majority for whom freedom has
become a burden and a doubtful privilege. The famous 'scene'
at the foot of Mount Sinai (Ex.32) just before Moses brings
down the tables of the Law suddenly casts a revealing light on
the situation: the disgraceful breach of precisely this First
Commandment even before it has been solemnly promulgated.
Finding this freedom before God intolerably nebulous and
empty, an attempt is made to bring it closer to life, to make it
more concrete and tangible. The people dance around the
golden calf.

A precise historical account of what actually happened at the
foot of Mount Sinai is no longer possible. Some Old Testament
scholars interpret Exodus 32 as a backward projection of later
events which happened in the time of Jeraboam I and their
presentation in the form of an 'original apostasy supposed to
have taken place at the very moment of the revelation of God
at Sinai which was so constitutive for Israel'.[12] As a tangible
symbol of this apostasy, the 'golden calf' is an excellent choice.
It vividly portrays the various aspects of idolatry. The bull is
not only the 'embodiment of fertility' but symbolizes at the
same time military power and strength. It can also remind us of
the modern symbol of the 'golden calf' to denote the temptation to the worship of 'Mammon'.

This symbol captures some of the principles and under-
currents of paganism, or perhaps it would be less open to

misunderstanding to say of idolatry, old style and new: Firstly, in the field of *sexuality and fertility* which from the dawn of history down to our own times has provided an extremely powerful motive for a wide variety of religions. In the life of Israel's neighbouring peoples, it was omnipresent in the shape of the various cults devoted to Baal and Astarte; a form of religion which celebrated fertility in particular as the ultimate and supreme creative force which establishes and guarantees the life of nature and humanity. A particularly close connection is made here between sexuality and divinity, eros and religion. This conviction has again and again outlived the ancient, and characteristically diverse and changing forms, the gods and goddesses, and created new religions not only in antiquity but right down on into modern secular times. Even today there are many people who find in sexuality (if no longer in fertility) the ultimate promise and fulfilment for their personal life, in the hope of finding here in particular the final chance, the ultimate mystery which life can experience and celebrate; in other words, an authentically 'divine' dimension to life. This secular 'deification' of sexuality is amply illustrated in modern litera-ture and philosophy, as well as in the actual conduct of our contemporaries. On this view, the truly healing and redemptive power is to be sought in the instinctual life.

Then the 'golden calf' as a religious symbol for *military pwer* bent on conquest and domination. The situation here is much the same. Right throughout its history Israel was constantly confronted with very concrete forms of the worship of power. The deified rulers of Israel's imperial neighbours were not only a continual threat and challenge politically, but also theologi-cally, given the temptation to Israel also to adopt the 'religion' of these neighbours. Above all, the specific figure of the Pharaoh represented the 'house of bondage' from which Israel had been delivered not only because he was a political tyrant and an economic exploiter but also because he was a typical representative of a certain world-view, a religious cosmological system of values and approach to the world. I am thinking here of the 'ontocratic' system which prevailed in almost all the advanced religions and cultures of the East: a symbiosis of the divine with cultural and imperial power, and in consequence, the invocation of the divine cosmological order as guarantee of the dominant political interests. This was the 'idolatry' which confronted Israel in the shape of the Egyptians.

But this is true not only of the people of the Old Covenant but also of the Church, the people of the New Covenant, which is similarly tempted both from within and without. Think, for example, of the various power-structures of the 'Constantinian churches', an extremely dangerous form of idolatry right down to our own day, in which imperial or hierarchical power is idealized and ultimately divinized and all other concerns subordinated to this one single goal. Right down to our own times, too, this goal only seldom appears in all its nakedness, but typically, only in glorified religious and ideological forms. Think, for example, of the fascist mythology or the Stalinistic 'personality cults' and even, unfortunately, of certain 'messianic leaders' in the Third World. The 'golden calf' is therefore still alive and kicking in this form, as well, dazzling and destroying its devotees and its victims with undiminished seductive power.

The 'golden calf' is alive and dominant in a third sense, too (and this is the one most current in modern usage), namely as symbol of divinized economic power, symbol of money and capital, as the idol of the *Mammon-worshippers*. It is not, of course, in this sense that the 'scene' at Sinai is primarily to be understood. But it is striking how quickly even this form of idolatry is attacked and exposed already in the Old Testament, in the message of the prophets. It is in the New Testament, however, and particularly in the message of Jesus, that Mammon appears even more clearly as *the most dangerous idol* of all. The disciples of Jesus, at any rate, are summoned to make a final clear-cut decision here in respect of Mammon: 'No one can serve two masters . . . You cannot serve God and Mammon' (Mt.6:24). The apostle adds: 'the love of money is the root of all kinds of evil' (1 Tim.6:10). But it was the context of 'Christian civilization' that this form of idolatry in particular established itself ever more widely as the almost omnicompetent power. Money, gold, capital became and become for many, many people the one really fascinating attraction, the underlying concern giving life its meaning, i.e. an idol. This is 'writ large' in the ruthless concentration of the economic system on profit and the acquisition of power, with the con-

comitant exploitation of the economically weak and dependent. This 'dance around the golden calf' has been analyzed by
Karl Marx, among others, right down to its underlying
structures in modes of production and living conditions and
exposed as the basic constitution of the capitalist system. But it
is also 'writ small' in the attitudes of private individuals,
perhaps in a less noxious, more restrained, more pragmatically
tenacious form. 'To have something is to be somebody', the
saying goes (or perhaps we should say 'works'). Not just
according to Marx but also according to Christian conviction,
one of the basic forms of human alienation is embodied in this
placing of 'possession' above 'being', in self-fulfilment through
the accumulation of capital, in the worship of money. The
'dance around the golden calf' is in this sense a quite contemporary idolatry and not indeed as something exceptional
and occasional but as something which is deeply ingrained in
society's most settled ways.

Idolatry as Debasement of the Currency

With loose reference to the term 'golden calf', I have touched
on just a few of the basic forms of idolatry ancient and modern.
There are many others. 'Idolatry' is a chapter of astonishing
richness in the phenomenology of religion. The number of
religions which have sprung up here is legion. The number of
religions which could still develop here is also legion. The
Reformers rightly pointed out that both individually and col-
lectively human beings have in this respect a quite inexhaust-
ible potentiality, and they spoke of the human heart as a
'veritable factory of idols'. But this industry is not limited to the
religious field. Production proceeds apace in every area and
aspect of life. While 'idolatry' is primarily a religious category,
the underlying tendency to elevate some aspect or power of
nature or culture to the status of the ultimate controlling factor
which gives meaning to life, and so to absolutize it, to idolize it,
can surface anywhere. In this sense, anything in our world can
become an idol, something 'divine', 'another god'. These are
very questionable and yet very real phenomena. For thinking
as well as thoughtless people, every 'penultimate' can become
an 'ultimate', which is precisely what the Bible means by
idolatry.

The temptation to idolatry is vigorously rejected in the First Commandment (and in the two commandments which follow). 'You shall have no other gods before me!' The Commandment does not deny the existence and influence of these 'other gods', these other forces in nature, history and society. To repeat what was said earlier, it is much more concerned with a clear-cut monolatry than with rational monotheism (though this, too, is quite in order). The biblical faith is inconceivable without this restriction: unconditional obedience, undivided respect, or, in the words of Jesus, love 'with all your heart, with all your soul, and with all your mind' (Mt.22:37) is due *only* to the One who is named. In our human life, only in relation to God is this element of the unconditional and the ultimate appropriate. *Soli Deo gloria* – To God alone the glory!

This is undoubtedly a 'hard saying'. It runs counter to well-known tendencies in our human nature and culture. (The intimate connection between 'culture' and 'cult' is already apparent in the terms themselves.) We are very reluctant to accept an unconditional claim of this kind. We take no pleasure in disowning the idols we find so attractive. There are vivid illustrations of this throughout the Old Testament. Even characters who are closely connected with the history of the promise try to smuggle their idols through the customs barrier. Think only of the story of Rachel in Gen.31:19ff.! Religiously inclined human beings, in particular, seem to find the categorical imperative of the First Commandment too intolerant and impoverishing, a demand for 'religious asceticism'.

I would not wish to deny that this asceticism can be misconceived and misinterpreted in a very narrowminded and blinkered fashion. An illustration of this danger can be found in my own Reformed tradition with its traditional distrust not just of idols but also of many cultural forms. In seeking to guard against the idolatrous spirit, people distrust the areas of human life which provide the occasion for it – the areas of sexuality and art, for example, (though not so much those of power and finance!). But even from the standpoint of the Old Testament, indeed, especially from its standpoint, such a simplistic attitude must be strongly challenged. It is never permissible to play the Creator off against the creation. The conflict is between Yahweh and deified powers. And *here* faith summons us to a definite choice, either the one or the other but not both. But we cannot extend the rejection of the idols to include also the areas from which they are fabricated, by an inadmissible absolutization and worship. On the contrary, the renunciation of the idols liberates creation and its forces for rational human use and control and in this sense for our 'reasonable service'. The concentration required by religious asceticism, far from being an end in itself, is simply the way to a truly creaturely, rational and, above all, free attitude to the values and gifts of nature and culture in our human world.

This does not mean a devaluation of nature and the created world but their 'demythologization' in the interests of freedom. For even the highest values and aspects of creation become a stumbling block and a house of bondage for humanity when they are divinized and idolized. To take the three examples suggested by the symbol of the golden calf: Human sexuality is certainly an excellent and creative gift but if it is made the dominant interest in life to the exclusion of all other interests, if it becomes a secular form of salvation, it becomes destructive and enslaving. When politics is turned into a 'religion' and becomes not a penultimate but an ultimate concern and, above all, when dictatorial power, the 'cult of personality', becomes an end in itself, life in the political realm is alienated and dehumanized. The deceit and inhumanity of absolutized money are equally evident, and this not only in its victims, whose scope for living is diminished by the lust of others for profit, but also in the profiteers themselves, since, in the last analysis, who is more a slave than the devotee of Mammon?! When 'having' is made absolute, real 'being' is destroyed. This is the inner logic of idolatry: the idols enslave those who put their trust in them, diminish the humanity of their devotees and in the end betray them. The idols cannot deliver what they promise; they cannot give meaning and purpose to human life. On the contrary, they bar the way to life in true freedom and openness.

The purpose of the First Commandment is to arm us against this dangerous temptation. 'You shall have no other gods before me!' Recall once again the context. This command is addressed to the newly liberated people. It is concerned with their newly acquired freedom. It commands them to *live* in this freedom and not to sell their 'birthright' for a 'mess of pottage' which is all that idolatries, ancient and modern, have to offer. This, then, is the 'narrow' way of the First Commandment, the 'narrow' way of the Exodus, the departure from the 'godless bond' into the covenant of freedom, the departure for the open country at the bidding of the sovereign, supreme, pioneering, trail-blazing God 'who brought them out of the land of Egypt, out of the house of bondage.'

Soli Deo Gloria

At the outset of these reflections I referred to the dominant role played by this First Commandment in Luther's exposition of the Decalogue in his *Small Catechism*. But the famous motto of the Genevan Reformation – *Soli Deo gloria* – also reflects this basic thrust of the First Commandment. In the opening questions of his *Geneval Catechism* (1541), Calvin already links the question of 'the chief end of human life' with the purpose of God 'to be glorified in us' and 'that our life . . . should be devoted to His glory'.[13] In the last analysis, this is what the Christian life is all about – giving God alone the glory. This orientation of doctrine and life – based on the First Commandment, among other biblical indications – left an indelible mark on the whole of Reformed theology and ethics.

Both within and outside the Reformed tradition, this principle of *Soli Deo gloria* has often been misinterpreted to mean a rigid and ultimately abstract theocentrism. Are not theocratic (and even authoriatarian) tendencies to be found in Calvin and his followers? Did this not lead to and encourage a pattern of thought which insisted on the 'from above'? It can hardly be denied that such temptations existed in the Protestant tradition. But if we begin with this First Commandment, we are helped to discover another possibility embedded in the approach and interpretation adopted in the Reformed tradition, namely, its essentially emancipatory thrust and influence, liberating both ethically and politically. Glory is to be ascribed not to just any abstract 'God' we can devise for ourselves but only to 'Yahweh', to the God 'who brought you out of the land of Egypt, out of the house of bondage'. Only to the God of the covenant history is glory due. The dominant interest of this

history is not naked sovereignty but our liberation and freedom.

There are tangible traces of the ethically and politically
liberating influence of this Reformed emphasis on the *Soli Deo
gloria* in history. It is certainly no accident that so many
genuinely liberating political (specifically 'democratic') initiatives should have been launched under this particular banner.
If the glory is God's alone, then no earthly authority can claim
this ultimate glory for itself. Where the sovereignty of God and
the lordship of Jesus Christ are emphasised, we have an
effective counterpoise to all forms of political absolutism and
totalitarianism. Under this banner, no political ruler is to be
followed blindly. If we fear God, we have no cause to fear any
earthly ruler (as John Knox for one was tireless in proclaiming
and practising!).

The First Commandment provides a warrant for a concentration on the 'glory of God' which opens up the human sphere for
adult 'participation' and cooperation on the part of the people
of God – a promise and also a task, that of demonstrating the
relevance of the First Commandment in church and society
even today.

From Image to Divine Name

An Israelite Peculiarity?

'You shall not make for yourself a graven image, or any likeness . . . you shall not bow down to them or serve them.' In the history of exegesis, the close connection between the Second Commandment and the First has constantly been emphasised. Indeed, so much so, that in some confessional traditions the Second Commandment has been regarded simply as a commentary on the first and very often even omitted altogether. This devaluation of the Second Commandment must be resisted, I believe. Like all those that follow it, the Second Commandment, though inseparably connected with the First, is not completely swallowed up by it. In this Second Commandment, the overriding concern to give God alone the glory – *Soli Deo gloria* – is brought to a sharp focus and given a thrust which needs to be remembered in theology and ethics.

The special significance of the Second Commandment is clear from the biblical theological context. The prohibition of images is a central element in the faith of the Old Testament; it forms part of what is distinctively biblical over against most other religions. The theological content of this Second Commandment has been very closely studied by Old Testament scholars in recent times, in particular by Gerhard von Rad. It is not a new discovery, of course, that the people of Israel was clearly differentiated from its neighbours in this particular respect, and became the 'odd man out', the 'stranger' in that multicoloured world of religions where, of course, the worship of images played a preponderant role. This Israelite peculiarity provoked sharp reactions from the surrounding world which rejected it as 'Jewish barbarism' and even as 'atheism'. Yet in the period of the Enlightenment, for example, the rationalist interpreters of religion also admired it as one of the particular merits of Old Testament religion. What is fairly new is the attempt to define more precisely the theological drift and thrust of this Second Commandment and to explain more fully its *Sitz im Leben* in the Old Testament faith.

This immediately rules out one popular misinterpretation of the Second Commandment, in particular, which has often been encouraged not only in traditional but also in modern exegesis, namely, the idealistic interpretation. 'Starting from an antithesis between visible and invisible, material and spiritual, which, while quite generally held, is quite alien to the Old Testament, the critics thought that the Second Commandment had to be understood as the expression of a special spirituality in the worship of God, as the signal, important defeat of a sipirtual and cultic primitivism, and so as the attainment of a decisive stage in the education of the human race.'[14] On this view, the Second Commandment was a plea for a purely spiritual, abstract view of God.

Von Rad rightly described such a view as 'dangerous' and 'completely erroneous'. It distorts the meaning of the commandment. The last thing the Decalogue is concerned with is an abstract, spiritualized view, a 'pure concept', of God. It starts right away with the introduction of God's name in the context of a quite concrete historical gift and blessing: the deliverance from bondage in Egypt. Nor is God spoken of in any abstract and generalised way in the Second Commandment, far from it, but in vivid and intense terms: he is a 'jealous God, visiting the iniquity of the fathers upon the children to the third and fourth generations . . . but showing steadfast love to thousands . . .' The same applies to the Bible as a whole. It dares to speak of God in an unreservedly vivid and graphic way, in 'narrative' terms and therefore, pictorially, even in deliberately anthropomorphic terms. The intention of the text of the Second Commandment cannot be to prohibit us from speaking of God in graphic earthy language and imagery, therefore. Nor is there any unqualified call to iconoclasm, requiring us to be suspicious of everything material and concrete in worship and life. Such interpretations of the Second Commandment – of which clear traces are found in the Reformed tradition (the mistrust of the plastic arts, for example) – completely mistake the real intention of the Decalogue.

Safeguard against the encroachments of image-making

We must be at once more cautious and more radical in interpreting this intention of the Decalogue. We must be careful not to ignore the fact that what the Second Command- ment prohibits is not all images and all image-making (the plastic arts) but only the religious or ideological transfiguration of images and pictures into *cultic* objects. 'You shall not *bow down* to them nor *serve* them!' The protest here is against the misuse not the use of the plastic arts (in both the literal and the wider sense). But we must also be more radical in our under- standing of this prohibition. The command is not concerned with the perpetuation of a liturgical peculiarity of Israelite worship but with the integrity of the Exodus faith in all its essential dimensions: in its understanding of the world, of God, and of humanity. We shall look briefly at each of these three dimensions.

1. The inseparable connection between the Second Com- mandment and the Old Testament *view of the world* is strongly emphasised by von Rad in his reflections on the prohibition of images in the Old Testament, to which reference has already been made. It is from this standpoint, indeed, that he seeks to interpret the biblical doctrine of creation. He sees this, so to speak, as the logical corollary of the Second Commandment, just as, conversely, he seeks to discover the intention of the Second Commandment in the context of the doctrine of crea- tion. In the biblical view of creation, God is God and world is world. There is no natural or supernatural merger or fusion of the two. As creation, the world is not divine but a created reality. As Creator, God is not a piece, not even the best or the worthiest piece of the world. The corollary of this is that it is impossible to capture and conceive of God in the forms of the world. Yet it was precisely in this direction that the cult of images in the peoples around Israel tended. Images seemed to guarantee the presence of the divinity in the world of nature and in human society. The boundary between God and world was blurred. God became transparent and tangible in a piece of the world. And pieces of the world came to be regarded as divine.

The Israelites were distinguished from their neighbours by a

radically different view of the world. A choice had to be made
between a theological and a mythological view of the world,
between Yahweh the Creator and 'divine' powers of nature
and culture. This was the fundamental decision of faith, and
cultic practice provided the test case. This explains why Israel
took this Second Commandment so seriously and why, as
would also happen later in the history of the Church, on this
issue in particular, it was ready in obedience to this commandment, to make it a *status confessionis,* a matter of confession
even to the point of martyrdom. Clearly this was not a question
merely of some liturgical innovation but a fundamental religious decision.

2. Biblical faith is faith in God. What is at stake here in the
Second Commandment, therefore, at the same time and above
all, inseparably bound up with Israel's view of the world, is
Israel's *view of God.* God cannot be imprisoned in the forms of
this world. He is the free and sovereign Lord of his creation,
and beyond creation's control. The Second Commandment
affirms God's sovereignity, or, better, his freedom *vis-à-vis* the
creation. The *'Soli Deo gloria'* of the First Commandment is
sharply focussed here in the affirmation that God cannot be
taken captive. No image and no mental concept can capture
him. No cultic practice and no place of worship can guarantee
his presence. No institution or movement 'possesses' him.
There are no automatic methods of 'manipulating' him.

The Second Commandment causes a quite unparalleled dis-
turbance within the history of Israel, therefore. 'The relentless
shattering of cherished concepts of God which occupied the
pre-exilic prophets stands in a theological relationship which is
perhaps hidden but which is, in actual fact, very close to the
commandment prohibiting images.'[15] This Commandment also
provides Christian theology with a powerful stimulus to reflection; indeed, more than a stimulus, rather a permanent explosive charge is implanted by it within all its doctrinal systems.
This Commandment counters every attempt to stabilize the
doctrine of God, a constant temptation for all church
theologians. *'Deus semper maior'* (God is always greater): this
dogmatic maxim of the Church Fathers catches the spirit of the
prohibition of images, the cutting edge of which we are so often
tempted to soften.

3. The Second Commandment strives for the greater glory of God. But, biblically, this means also and at the same time, for the greater glory of the *human creature*. It may seem a little risky to be already thinking of human affairs in the context of the commands of the First Table. But, as I understand the matter, we are clearly justified in doing so. We are encouraged to do so not only in virtue of central christological arguments (since in the light of the history of Jesus Christ, God and humanity are in 'covenant') but also on the basis of the Decalogue itself. Just as the Second Table cannot be separated from the First, so neither the First from the Second. This prohibition of images is also of vital importance for our human relationships with one another.

We human beings have a notorious and almost incorrigible tendency to 'image making' in relation to our neighbours. We make our own images of them, seek to 'capture' them, take possession of them, to define for ourselves and for them what they 'really' are. This is not in itself reprehensible. Human life would be impossible for us if we did not have ideas of one another. We project and develop images – human images, too, human images especially. Here again, this enterprise becomes dangerous and even fatal only when we 'bow down' to these images we have made and worship them, i.e. make a 'fetish' of them and fit our fellow human beings to these caricatures so as to manipulate them for our own purposes.

Our human life is endangered by such conduct in great matters and in small. In great matters: we think here of the 'battlefields' of the ideologies and of advertising, in both East and West. Take for example, the way in which East European educational policy is constantly trying to impose certain pre-conceived ideas about humanity and even (atheistic) images of God on society. The socialist citizen has to conform to these caricatures and the discriminatory consequences of not conforming to them are only too well-known. But similar tendencies are also found in the West, though here the considerations are not so much political and ideological as economic and technocratic. Think of the daily pressures exercised by advertising, with its 'hidden persuaders' and insidiously seductive images which seek to condition consumers and citizens so that they may be more amenable to exploitation in certain directions.

But similar tendencies are also to be found in the small matters, too, in our concrete everyday relationships. We project images of our fellow human beings and they of us. We already know what they (and we) already are. Bert Brecht summed up this tendency in the following anecdote: ' "What do you do when you love a person?", Mr. K. was asked. "I make myself a mental image", Mr. K. replied, "and try for a good likeness". "The image?" "No", said Mr. K., "the person".'[16] Caricatures of this sort obstruct our real access to one another and diminish our mutual human freedom, just as God's freedom is endangered when we make a fetish of our theological images and concepts. Such absolutized images also entail a loss of real humanity.

It is here, I believe, that we discover the abiding and even enhanced relevance of the Second Commandment today. This command defends God and ourselves from attempts to control us by manipulative 'image making'. In the interests of God's freedom and our own, it opposes all control of this kind. Expressed in positive terms, developed and given concrete content in the New Testament, it is a summons to the practice of patient, inventive and imaginative love. By the pressure it exercises on us in the direction of the concrete, the personal, the dynamic, this love is the most effective antidote to the kind of image making which establishes rigid stereotypes.

Max Frisch provides a vivid commentary on this aspect of the Second Commandment in his Diary of the years 1946 to 1949. I quote two passages illustrating both the fatal and the liberating role of images. The first is a very homely example drawn from the life of the diarist's mother: 'Even some fixed opinion held by our friends, parents, or teachers, can weigh on many with the force of an ancient oracle . . . Not that the prophecy need necessarily be fulfilled literally; even when it is resisted its influence can still be discerned in our very refusal to conform to the picture others have us . . . A schoolteacher once told my mother that she would never learn to knit. My mother often told us of this prophecy. She had never forgotten it, never forgiven it. She became and enthusiastic and exceptionally skilled knitter, and all the socks and caps, gloves and pullovers I ever possessed, I owed in the last analysis to this unwelcome prophecy!'[17]

Then, secondly, Max Frisch pays the following tribute to the liberating power of love: 'The strange thing is that it is those we love whom we find hardest to define. But this is precisely what love, the miraculous thing in love, is: the way it keeps us in a living state of suspense, ready to follow a person through all possible developments ... Love releases us from every portrait. The exciting, adventurous, really breathtaking thing about love is that we can never master the loved one, just because, and as long as, we love them ... The loved one is rich with every possibility, rich in mysteries, inconceivable ...'[18]

How does God become concrete?

Let me try to sum up what we have learned from these three arguments. In his book on the Ten Commandments, Gerhard Ebeling introduces his study of the Second Commandment with the question: 'How does God become concrete?'[19] By this creative approach to the problem he guards against the idealistic misunderstanding of the comandment to which reference was made earlier. What the Second Commandment is affirming – in contrast to the vivid and colourful idolatry practised in the world around Israel – is not the same 'abstract' generalized view of God, but God in his true concreteness.

This has both a negative and a positive implication. God is not 'concrete' in the manner in which such concreteness is thought of in the crude or subtle 'image theology' of Israel's neighbours. God does not become tangible in 'holy things'. From the biblical standpoint, such a view of God is 'pseudo-concrete' rather than concrete. By imprisoning God in images, we make him part of the world of already given realities. But from the biblical standpoint, God is concrete only in his voluntary self-giving, in his love, in his free judgement and sovereign grace (of which this Second Commandment, in particular, speaks so emphatically).

In the New Testament, the question 'How does God become concrete?' receives its final answer and fulfilment in the history of Jesus Christ, which continues the whole thrust of the Second Commandment. In the basic theological theme of this history, in the 'Gospel of God's way to humanity' (as J. L. Hromadka used to call it), there is an astonishing concreteness and palpability in the things that happen and in the way they happen: the concreteness of the life and the sufferings of Jesus, his unqualified sharing of our actual human lot, and even the vivid realism of his teaching – think of his parables and the way they incorporate our tiny human world into the great world of God. From the New testament standpoint, this is how we are to understand God: in the history of his incarnation, in his entry into our ordinary mundane human world.

This is how God becomes concrete. It is significant that the only legitimate 'image of God' to be found in the 'New Testament is in the 'face of Jesus Christ' (2 Cor.4:4,6; Col.1:15). If the question of God's concreteness is to be answered in accord with the Second Commandment, it is to this history of Jesus Christ that we must look. Away from images to the *'Ecce homo!'* of the New Testament – this is the Christian significance of the Second Commandment.

Ebeling is surely right when he sums up the whole matter in these words: 'To idolize human beings is the worst kind of idolatry. But to believe in the presence of God in our fellow human beings, to take them seriously as the image of God, as God's representatives, to give concrete expression to the reverence, love and trust which we owe to God in our dealings with them, this is the purest form of the worship and service of God.'[20]

Against the Misuse of God's Name

'You shall not take the name of the Lord your God in vain; for the Lord will not hold guiltless anyone who takes his name in vain.' This Third Commandment also follows the direction which gives the first three commandments their essential coherence. It, too, is concerned above all with the honour and glory of God: *Soli Deo gloria!* Between the Second and Third Commandments the connection is especially close, which is why I deal with them together in this chapter. Unless I am much mistaken, we are dealing here with two aspects of one and the same directive, one and the same movement away from images of God to the name of God, away from a false and enslaving approach to God in the direction of a true and liberating worship and service of God. But what actually is the

aspect of God's glory which is given concrete expression in this Third Commandment?

It is not easy to grasp the relevance of the Third Commandment in the contemporary ethical context. More than in the case of the other commandments, its application to life seems obscured by changed circumstances. Helped by the findings of Old Testament scholarship we can to some extent establish its original setting. Its background seems to have been the protest against any misuse of the divine name in sorcery; i.e. against the manipulation of the name 'Yahweh' for magical purposes, a temptation which was all too frequently present and yielded to among Israel's neighbours and one which even in Israel was a constant danger.

In addition, however, we must also think of the danger of perjury since 'every genuine oath was accompanied by the invocation of the deity':[21] A false oath was not only a lie in human eyes but also in God's eyes. Here again, the two Tables of the Law are intimately related. It is also a well-known fact that anxiety lest the divine name be misused even in less serious circumstances led in the later history of Israel to an almost complete abhorrence of uttering the divine name 'Yahweh' at all and to the custom of substituting the term 'Adonai' for it. Something of this abhorrence remained in the traditional exposition of the Commandment in the form of warnings to Christians not to utter the name of God (or Jesus) thoughtlessly and frivolously. But such sins are surely mere peccadilloes today, 'puppet sins' (as Luther called them), offences of only marginal interest to society, even if fresh life can sometimes be infused into them, as can be seen from the recurring waves of interest in magic even today. But in terms of the mainstream of our life, this is hardly our problem today. The following comment of one of the most recent writers on the Decalogue comes as no surprise: 'What is typical of us is not the misuse of God's name but the fact that we no longer use it at all. The divine name is like an old coin which has been withdrawn from circulation.'[22]

But when we understand its central thrust, even this Third Commandment still has its permanent validity. To see this, all we need to do is to dig below its surface meaning or its historical reference. Above all, we have to reflect on the significance of the divine name in the Bible. This name is certainly no mere arbitrary *flatus vocis,* mere 'sound and fury, signifying nothing'. The problem is not one to be solved merely in terms of utterance or non-utterance. From the biblical standpoint, the name is the message, the authoritative promise and fulfilment of the reality denoted by and revealed in the name. Recall the presentation of the name 'Yahweh' in the Preamble to the Decalogue, where it stands for the promise of freedom, the recollection of the Exodus, and the new life oriented towards hope. The name 'Yahweh' is itself taken to mean 'I will be what I will be' or 'I will be there to help you', i.e. is itself sufficient ground for striking camp and setting forth.

In the light of this, the misuse of the divine name would seem to me to have a deeper significance: it is the *refusal to follow and obey God.* And this is the classic sin of the people of God. The threat to Israel and to the Church here stems from within rather than from without, as in the Second Commandment. For the people of God, life is life in God's name. 'Theologically' this name 'takes the place which in other cults was occupied by the cultic image'.[23] The hope of the people of God is anchored in this name. At the same time, however, there is also here the temptation to name the name of God, the name of Jesus, without taking seriously what the name stands for; to appeal to the Exodus or the history of Christ but not to be committed to them, no to act accordingly, not to accept their implications. We say 'Lord! Lord!' but fail to do his will. At the very worst, and here the magical elements come into view, we shelter behind the name of God, using it as a pretext and an automatic insurance for our own interests.

To misuse the name of God means, therefore, that instead of placing ourselves at God's disposal we place him at ours, domesticating his holy name for our unholy or pseudo-holy purposes. The God of liberation is turned into a domestic deity, a household god.

It is no accident that the theologians who made this aspect of the Third Commandment the operative centre of their utterances were in the main those who were socially alert, such as the Christian socialists. For example, Leonhard Ragaz stressed in his cathechism: 'One thing is supremely important: Is our relationship to God one of service to him, or do we try to use

God to serve our own ends?'[24] Nothing is more perverse than selfishness in the guise of religion; we try to make God the servant of our purely secular ambitions, as communities, churches or nations, races or religions, or else the servant of our individual ambitions, our lust for position and power.

But there are also more subtle ways of misusing God's name, ways which are not overtly but disguisedly and evasively hypocritical ways of refusing to follow and obey God, by putting certain areas of human life out of bounds to the divine name. Here the Exodus faith is turned into a private affair.

Ragaz is penetrating here, too: 'We also misuse God's name when we acknowledge God for our private ends alone and fail to ask whether his will is also done in the whole world, in political and social matters, in life as a whole'.[25] Here the classic temptation of the people of God smoulders beneath the surface, less obtrusively, not so manifestly perverse, yet for that very reason *the* temptation in church history. It is to *this* temptation that our attention is directed by the Third Commandment.

I do not believe that this extension of the scope of the Third Commandment is an illegitimate widening of its original reference. The fact is that the historical context of the Exodus history suggests this extension. The East German theologian H. G. Fritzsche provides us with a helpful pointer in this direction. He even goes so far as to suggest that substantial support for this extension can already be found in the original meaning of this Commandment. He interprets the Commandment against the background of the occupation of the promised land. The event of the Exodus is here completed and rounded off: 'The union established for the journey (from Egypt to Canaan) is dissolved. Everyone departs "to his own tent", to his own home and farmstead. Metaphorically, everyone is "demobbed" and returns to "civvy street". This situation produced one of the most serious crises of Israelite faith, for Yahweh the God of Israel is originally and essentially the God of the *people* of Israel . . . The danger now threatening is that the people will desert to the gods – essentially private gods – of the now captured land of Canaan, and so fall into superstition and idolatry, or even that Yahweh himself will come to be understood in the same way that these private Canaanite gods were understood and, therefore, as unconcerned with the cause of the whole people of Israel, regarded merely as an individual support and talisman'.[26] It is to this temptation that the Third Commandment is opposed and provides help to resist and overcome.

Leaving on one side the question whether this view of the context of the Third Commandment is correct in every detail, I am persuaded that it provides a valid key to the understanding of both the ancient and modern relevance of the Commandment. Like the first petition of the Lord's prayer 'Hallowed be thy name' in its positive sense, the Third Commandment challenges us as to the integrity of our faith. It assumes that each of us and the whole Church is serious about the faith we profess and protects us against any schizophrenic dividing our words from our deeds, our justification from justice, grace from obedience. The name of God and the history of God are inextricably and inseparably linked. If this name is not hallowed in the fulfilment of this history, in practical obedience, then it is misused, taken in vain. This is the ethical implication of the Third Commandment. It is here that the credibility of our life as Christians and the Church is decided, and this is a matter which the Bible treats with the utmost seriousness. The extremely solemn warning given in this Commandment in particular – 'For the Lord will not hold anyone guiltless who takes his name in vain' – and addressed quite unmistakably to believers, is not accidental. Once freedom is opened up to us and grace offered to us – and this is the ultimate and overriding vista of the Decalogue and of the Third Commandment – treating responsibility and judgement lightly is quite out of the question.

THE FOURTH COMMANDMENT:

The Festival of Freedom

Disciplinary Measure or Invitation to Freedom?

'The Festival of Freedom'!? This may seem a rather outlandish title to give to an attempt to interpret the Fourth Commandment, the injunction to keep holy the Sabbath day. Is this really what the Fourth Commandment is about? Of all the commandments this one in particular is focussed on a specific matter. It provides the rule for a specific day and thus prescribes a quite specific style of life. The aim of the other commandments is to establish more general rules for daily life and conduct and therefore leave greater room for our human response. Here in the Fourth Commandment, on the contrary, we seem to be driven into a narrow space and our attention is directed to one particular day. There is no escaping the feeling that instructions are being given and rules laid down. Quite clearly a discipline is being imposed here on the people of God. But for adult people, discipline and rules often represent neither a festival nor freedom.

The history of the Fourth Commandment and its application shows quite clearly that these misgivings about it have not been gratuitously invented. In the case of no other commandment has interpretation and practice been so casuistical and paternalistic as here in the case of the Fourth Commandment. The attitude to the Sabbath in Judaism in the lifetime of Jesus is one example. An attempt was made to control the content and form of the seventh day down to the very last detail by grotesquely complicated regulations, and to use every available moral pressure and administrative measure to force people to take these regulations seriously. Not surprisingly, therefore, the sharpest and bitterest conflicts between Jesus and the scribes of his day were focussed on this Fourth Commandment.

It was in this context that Jesus spoke of 'straining at a gnat and swallowing a camel' (Mt.23:24). For those, therefore, who, because of their ignorance or position in society, were in no position to understand the complicated details of this mass of regulations, a day so burdened with legal provisions, far from being a 'festival of freedom' was a sinister, even a terrifying day, a *Dies ater!*

Not that Christians are in any position to look down condescendingly on this development within Judaism (which in any case was an aberration capable of correction). The Fourth Commandment often became a veritable goldmine for the legalists and the 'Sabbath' turned into a day dominated by strict rules and discipline even in the history of Christianity. This applies to the Reformed tradition especially. The Reformed fathers (rightly) attached great importance to the Fourth Commandment, yet managed to hamstring it in their very enthusiasm for it. We need only recall the relentless sabbatarianism of the Anglo-Saxon Puritans and their rigorously Puritanical theory and practice of 'Sabbath' observance, their rigid opposition to all worldly occupations and games and amusements on Sundays, which had to be devoted exclusively to worship. We still come across traces of this even today, in Scotland, for example, the classic country of the Calvinist Reformation. But the same thing used also to be found in other Reformed cities such as Basle, only here the liberalizing process which accompanied the increasing secularization got off to an earlier start and proved more effective.

It is significant that Karl Barth begins his doctrine of creation with a chapter on 'The Holy Day'. With conditions in 18th century Basle in mind he says: 'To be sure, we must not overlook the good intentions of the Sabbath ethics of the older Reformed Church. But the fact that it is so blatantly adapted to the requirements and claims of the ruling classes betrays only too clearly that a system of human rules is here being substituted for God's command, with disastrous consequences. It is not surprising that this sort of Sunday could not assert itself either in the lower or upper classes of European humanity in face of the growing pressures of modern secularism.'[27] It is only right to add that the secularized 'emancipation' of the Sunday familiar to us today, far from bringing real freedom, has very often only resulted in an 'unleashing' of life-styles which engender different forms of oppression. Think of the modern 'leisure industry', the carnage on the roads on major public holidays, the 'lost (i.e. aimless and wasted) weekends' which with good reason seem even more meaningless than alienated 'working days'.

In view of these aspects of religious and secular history, to speak of a 'festival of freedom' does seem quite far-fetched. Yet the abuse of a good custom does not cancel out its proper use. This Fourth Commandment has another aspect, it offers another possibility. I am thinking here not only of other, incomparably more positive aspects of the theoretical and practical influence of the Fourth Commandment in church and society, though this, too, should not be ignored. We must endorse Th. Zahn's verdict on the cultural influence of Christianity in his 'Sketches from the life of the early Church': 'There are familiar social institutions and patterns which are generally recognized not only as undoubtedly Christian in origin but also as having had beneficial effects right down to our own time. One of the most important of these institutions is the Sunday holiday. The heathen world had no Sunday. Neither the peoples of classical antiquity nor our barbarian ancestors had any such holiday recurring regularly at short intervals'.[28] Zahn needs to be corrected on one point: the Sunday as a holiday, as a day of festival, was not a Christian innovation but derived from the Old Testament Sabbath commandment. But recognizing this derivation, it still remains a unique contribution of the biblical tradition to the history of our civilization, one which, unparalleled in respect of its Israelite source, has influenced the whole world, at least in the sense that most people today take for granted the need for a regularly recurring 'day of rest'.[29] The opportunity which this implies for freedom and which still remains open to us in spite of the abuses to which it is open, should certainly not be underestimated.

But in speaking of the 'festival of freedom' I am not thinking mainly of this historical influence of the Fourth Commandment but rather of its original meaning and purpose. I want to look now at this latter theme, and to do so in two stages: first, its context in biblical theology, and secondly, the ethical implications of the Sabbath and Sunday commandment.

The Two Versions of the Fourth Commandment

In the overwhelming opinion of recent Old Testament scholarship, the Fourth Commandment in particular is the strongest argument in support of the view that 'in its original form at least, the Decalogue . . . very probably dates from the Mosaic period'.[30] It is in that period, therefore, in the Exodus and the events of the covenant, that its original theological basis is also to be sought. What was affirmed earlier with respect to the Decalogue as a whole is confirmed in this commandment in particular: the Sabbath commandment is rooted in the covenant history of Yahweh. From the very beginning, therefore, the Sabbath is a festival of freedom. With Ernst Jenni we can say: 'Alongside the reminder of the jealous God . . . the reminder of the gracious Liberator is introduced in the observance of the Sabbath. The joyful character of this day, standing in such typical and welcome contrast to the Babylonian *umu limnu,* for example, with its complete insecurity in face of sinister forces despite the magical efforts of the priestly science, follows directly from this.'[31]

For the religion of Israel, this commandment was really basic. Theologically it is important to notice its different versions in order to grasp the different aspects of this 'festival of freedom'. In their agreement and their difference, two of these versions are particularly important, the Deuteronomic version (Deut.5:12ff.) and the Priestly version found in the classic passage (Ex.20). While the importance of the Fourth Commandment comes out very clearly in the two versions, a different explanation is given of it in each case. In the Deuteronomic version we are told: 'The seventh day is a sabbath to the Lord your God; in it you shall not do any work, you, or your son, or your daughter, or your manservant, or your maidservant, or your ox, or your ass, or any of your cattle, or the sojourner who is within your gates, that your manservant and your maidservant may rest as well as you. You shall remember that you were a servant in the land of Egypt and the Lord your God brought you out thence with a mighty hand and an outstretched arm; therefore the Lord God commanded you to keep the sabbath day.'

There are two clear emphases in this Deuteronomist explanation of the reasons for this commandment. In the first place, the commandment does not hang in the air or move in some timeless or abstract religious realm. It has its concrete setting in life: the Sabbath is *the day on which freedom is commemorated.* Certainly it is not just a backward looking day of commemoration but one which is relevant to the present. It is a day of commemoration with 'world changing consequences'. Which brings us to the second emphasis in this Deuteronomic explanation: the 'social dimension' of this day is very much to the forefront. Freedom is meant to be lived and practised. There is a distinctively evangelical note: not only one's own family is remembered but also one's neighbours, close and distant, and not even the animals are excluded; they too may join in this festival of freedom. But the really striking thing is the way the commandment focusses on the socially disadvantaged and oppressed; the benefits of this day are meant, above all, for the slaves (male and female). People who have themselves been liberated – who were themselves once slaves – must never forget that their freedom carries with it special responsibilities. The new step into freedom which the Exodus represented produces ripples, is meant to spread outwards in ever-widening circles. It may not be kept to oneself, reduced to a personal privilege, clutched to oneself. On the contrary, it is meant to bring relief to those especially who are most heavily burdened and this not as a display of an optional philanthropy but as a matter of inescapable divine right. Putting it in modern terms, it is not bestowed by society's rulers on the downtrodden as an 'act of clemency', i.e. as something which could be revoked at any moment, but as a divinely ordained 'pattern' of common human life in human – even creaturely – solidarity and fellowship. This is why this day is obligatory on all and liberating for all.

The explanation given in the Priestly version of the Fourth Commandment (Ex.20:11) points in a different direction. The seventh day is consecrated as a day of rest to the Lord your God, 'for in six days the Lord made heaven and earth, the sea and all that is in them, and rested the seventh day; therefore the Lord blessed the seventh day and hallowed it.' The argument here appeals to the creation, the creation story. The Priestly account of creation culminates, as you know, in the

creation sabbath. The theological significance of this is fundamental. Jenni comments: 'The work of creation is certainly
completed with the creation of humanity on the sixth day. But
the significant thing is that the creation story does not end here,
with the creation of humanity, the "crown of creation", the
creature which in its likeness to God is to continue the work of
creation in its own creaturely way. In other words, humanity
with its work and culture is still not the ultimate goal of God's
creation.'[32] Put in positive terms: 'The sabbath brings out the
truth that the creation, far from being an end in itself and left to
its own devices, finds its meaning only in fellowship with God.
The goal of creation is the praise of God offered by the whole
creation with humanity at its head.'[33] In this Priestly version the
sabbath commandment in an emphatic reminder of the
sovereignty of *God's free grace* as the alpha and omega of the
creation and, above all, of human life.

These two versions and explanations of the Fourth Commandment, labelled the 'social' and the 'cultic', or the
'anthropocentric' and the 'theocentric', have not only been
distinguished but even divorced and played off against each
other. In consequence people have also often gone completely
different ways in their theory and practice of the holy day. For
those who stressed the cultic and religious aspect, the sabbath
(the Sunday) naturally became a purely religious custom with a
strictly liturgical core, i.e. the day of worship in the narrower
sense, and in its distorted form even an El Dorado of legalistic
piety, indeed, even a 'confession of faith in their own Pharisa-
ism'.[34] The social dimensions of the sabbath remained merely
marginal, merely a 'by-product' of the holy day, with restrictions imposed more often than not on the very people who
needed this day's rest most because they worked the hardest
during the week. For the others, those who stressed the
humanitarian and social dimensions, the holy day became a
'holiday', simply a day of physical refreshment, relaxation and
enjoyment, a 'non-working' day. The 'rest of God' is lost sight
of altogether or else dismissed as no more than an occasional
marginal embellishment on special occasions. In the 'Christian
world' the observance of Sunday has hesitated indecisively
between these two poles. Today, of course, the pendulum is
swinging more in the second direction.

In my view, there is no need whatever to think here in terms of such stark alternatives. Neither the commandment itself requires us to do so nor is it called for in our practical obedience to the commandment. The two explanations are not mutually exclusive in the Bible. Certainly the Deuteronomist version stresses the social implications of the sabbath, but it does so in a pre-eminently theological context. Its argument rests squarely on the Exodus history and therefore looks towards Yahweh, 'who brought you out thence with a mighty hand and an outstretched arm.' The Priestly version, on the other hand, is thinking primarily of the great sabbath of God and so its approach is primarily theological. Yet in adopting this approach it certainly does not lose sight of the peace of the creation, the needs of the creation. It, too, mentions the fellow human being and the fellow creatures and does so with an inherent logic, for the grace of God the Creator shines out not in splendid isolation but in order to irradiate the creation and to come to the aid of His creatures in their distress. Here, too, therefore, wisdom suggests that we should respect the combination of the 'vertical' and the 'horizontal' which is so characteristic of the biblical way of thinking. In specific instances the emphasis may and should be placed differently but we are not to invent false alternatives. Concretely, picking up once again the formula 'the festival of freedom', if the Deuteronomist stresses that the sabbath is a festival of *freedom,* the Priestly theology stresses that it is the *festival* of freedom. The basic agreement supports, indeed requires, both emphases.

The Ethics of Sunday

It is along these lines, I believe, that we should approach the question of how we are to deal in practice with the 'holy day', i.e. the question of the *ethics of Sunday.* Certainly this question is not high on the agenda today. For most of our contemporaries it does not even arise. They take it for granted that they are free to pass this day (unlike their working days) just as they please and as the mood takes them. This is quite understandable, especially as a reaction against what happens on weekdays, which for most people are all too regimented and

monotonous. Nor is such an attitude surprising in itself if we
consider the cultic and religious legalism already referred to
which has so often been imposed on people in the history of the
Church up to now. On the other hand, if we try to let the
Fourth Commandment guide our ways, we must, rather we are
permitted, to add at once that the freedom with which this
'festival of freedom' is concerned includes *both* dimensions. It
is concerned with our temporal and physical human needs and
allows full scope to our psycho-physical *condition humaine*.
People are free to order their Sunday as a free day. When our
contemporaries actually choose to use this day in the way that
suits them, to sleep in (and so skip church attendance), to go
off on an outing, to potter around, to play or watch games, to
laze around or even to kill time, the reaction of the Church
should not be simply one of grim displeasure. There is one
radical saying of Jesus in the gospels which should by rights
have deprived church people of their fondness for complaints
on this score: 'The sabbath was made for human beings, not
human beings for the sabbath!' (Mk.2:27).

But when this human right is acknowledged, not just toler-
ated but positively affirmed, the biblical 'festival of freedom' at
once confronts us with a counter-question and the need for
more precision. What does this sabbath freedom really mean?
Is it no more than the freedom to follow our moods and
fancies? Is that really the last word or the only word to be said
about this freedom? More specifically, have we really rightly
understood the freedom of Sunday if we suppress or abandon
the 'Priestly' dimension of the sabbath, in other words, if we
discard or ignore the 'cultic', 'liturgical' reference to the 'rest'
and 'peace' disclosed to and bestowed on humanity in the
divine initiative and promised and offered to us in the celebration of this festival? To press the geometrical terminology once
more: is the festival of freedom really celebrated at all if it is
celebrated more or less exclusively in the horizontal dimension?

From the standpoint of the Fourth Commandment, particularly in its Priestly version, the answer to these questions is
clearly 'No'. It should be noted, however, that this 'No' is not in
the form of a 'vertical' counterblast to a 'horizontal' celebration of the Sunday nor of any assumed opposition between the

theological and anthropological dimensions. Nor is it a legalistic attitude. Behind the 'No' to these questions is an evangelical concern for genuine human freedom, for the ordering of this day in accordance with humanity's best interests. The positive meaning of this, according to the Fourth Commandment, is that the 'rest' we really need in our human life is more than psycho-physical recreation, however vital and important this concern may be. Understood in the light of the Fourth Commandment, this 'rest' is, in the last analysis, 'rest' in God's presence, the reminder of the beginning and end of our way, the rest *'sub specie aeternitatis'*. St. Augustine wrote imperishable words on this theme in his autobiography: of the 'restless heart' whose true 'rest' is to be sought only *coram Deo, donec requiescat in te*. And there is one important passage in the New Testament which views the Fourth Commandment from this eschatological perspective: the great passage in Hebrews 4 on the 'sabbath rest of God's people' where it is stated: 'So then, there remains a sabbath rest for the people of God; for whoever enters God's rest also ceases from his labours as God did from his' (Heb.4:10).

This opens up a dimension which cannot be ignored if we wish to do justice to the biblical view of the 'festival of freedom'. A theology which sought to conceal this dimension, either ashamed or perplexed because people nowadays do not ask this sort of question, would not only become 'savourless salt' but also fail those who are in fact seeking rest of this kind. For 'whether or not humanity finds rest or else is crushed by the burden of time does not depend on any outward apportionment of our time but our inner attitude to the *whole* of the time of our life'.[35] I referred earlier to the ambiguity of our use of leisure time and it needs to be mentioned again in the present context. 'Not just our working time but our leisure time, too, can become a crushing problem. Human beings are not necessarily more rested and better rested the more time they have for rest.'[36] The point to be stressed in the present context is the growing importance of this other 'Priestly' dimension of the Sunday for genuine human rest, quite apart from all the other sociological and psychological questions. At any rate, it appears more essential than ever today to keep these two dimensions of the Fourth Commandment together, even in tackling the practical questions of Sunday behaviour.

Brief mention must also be made here of the question of the *Sunday service* or, more precisely, of our participation in worship. It must only be a brief reference since I do not want to give the impression that the 'ethics of Sunday' ultimately boils down to the 'Sunday duty' in the sense of obligatory church going. It has often been understood in this way, of course, both in Reformed theology and in Catholic theology with its 'Sunday duty' of attendance at Mass. This narrow concentration on one particular aspect is to be resisted, especially when we fully understand the concern underlying it. The Fourth Commandment is all about a 'day of rest' and not just a churchgoing day. There is no mention at all of any obligatory church attendance. The early Church began by separating the two days, the sabbath, the day of rest, and the day of worship. It held its service of worship on the day of resurrection, i.e. the first day following the sabbath. Only later did it combine the two days, and this for compelling practical but not absolute reasons. People wanted to celebrate worship on their free day and Sunday was accordingly elevated to the status of a holiday. To treat the Sunday legalistically by insisting on obligatory worship is to misunderstand the Fourth Commandment, therefore. It seems to me no more appropriate to talk of a 'Sunday duty' than it would be to talk of a 'marriage duty' in Christian sexual ethics.

I would nevertheless want to maintain unequivocally that a Christian service of worship can and should be central and significant for the celebration of the festival of freedom. For the Christian service of worship is the time and the place for celebrating and practising the other fundamental dimension of the Sunday commandment, namely, its priestly dimension, where we focus on the beginning and end of our time and do so, indeed, not privately in an act of personal meditation, but in the fellowship of the Church and thus also demonstrate the 'social' dimension of the sabbath rest. For me, therefore, our participation in the prayer, singing, hearing and communion of the Church is an essential part of the Sunday celebration. I fully realize that our services of worship are often very disappointing in the form they take and that for outsiders they bear little resemblance to anything that might be called a 'festival of freedom'. I understand those, theologians included, who find this hard to take. What I fail to understand, however, is the permanent dispensation from participation in worship which some theologians accord themselves on this ground. No such dispensation is to be had on the basis of the Fourth Commandment. In the ethics of Sunday, participation in worship may not be a 'must' but it is certainly a 'may', an opportunity. We should not refuse to make use of this opportunity.

The Ethos of Anxiety, Industriousness and Success

The ethical implications of the Fourth Commandment have already been touched on in our reflections on the ordering of the Sunday, particularly in our comments on Christian worship. Certainly this needs to be done much more fully and in much greater depth than we have done so far. It may help us here to consider the status of the Fourth Commandment within the Decalogue as a whole. With its two dimensions, it very clearly binds the two tables of the Decalogue together. At the same time, however, it is also an important anticipation of the treatment of the other commandments concerned with the common life of humanity. Karl Barth was surely right to introduce his 'ethics of creation' with an interpretation of this Fourth Commandment. This sabbath rest of God and man is the basis of Christian ethical thought. And Christian ethics keeps this sabbath in its sights. To employ a central theological concept, the Christian ethic is to be understood, even and especially on the basis of the Decalogue, as an *ethic of grace*. It must be developed within the overall horizon of the 'festival of freedom'.

The practical implications of this characteristic of the Christian ethic will have to be demonstrated positively in my treatment of the commandments of the Second Table. In this closing section of the present chapter, however, I want to anticipate this positive demonstration by indicating *via negationis* what it does *not* mean, or rather, by differentiating it from certain contrasting types of ethical thinking: from the ethos of anxiety, industriousness and success. (I take the first two terms from H. G. Fritzsche, who employs them to denote the two conceptions which run counter to the Fourth Commandment.)

1. By the *'ethos of anxiety'* I mean a way of life dominated by the belief that we need to 'insure' ourselves, our family or our community, on a long term basis and against every conceivable danger; a way of life in which the future is viewed mainly and even exclusively as an obscure menace in which we must 'insure against' and 'provide for' in every way open to us. There is obviously a grain of truth in such an approach to life, both humanly and socially. The human being is a creature who 'looks ahead' and 'pro-vides'. Dependent as we are on our environment, we need to be provident. The forward planning of our individual and collective life can be a legitimate and central exercise of our human responsibility. The questionable 'ethos of anxiety' takes over at the point where planning assumes the perverted form of a desperate and ultimately enslaving effort to make ourselves secure independently and off our own bat. We have an illustration of this in Jesus' parable of the rich farmer (Lk.12:13-21). Here a man regards his wealth as his security, subordinates everything to this wealth as a final goal, toils for it, plans for it, builds for it. Finally he lets himself ease up; he has built and stocked enough barns to last him many years; he has made effective provision for his future. At last he can say: 'Soul, you have ample goods laid up for many years: take your ease, eat, drink and be merry.' But as a general rule of life, this 'ethos of anxiety' is a miscalculation which comes to grief on *la condition humaine;* it does *not* lead to 'rest': 'Fool! This night your soul is required of you . . .' (Lk.12:20).

The remedy for this 'anxiety', posited as the 'basic structure of existence' in the analyses conducted by Kierkegaard and Heidegger, for example, is provided by the Gospel and the Decalogue. From the Sermon on the Mount comes the clear call of Jesus: 'Do not be anxious about your life, what you shall eat or what you shall drink, nor about your body, what you shall put on. Is not life more than food, and the body than clothing? Look at the birds of the air . . .' (Mt.6:25ff). Certainly this is not an invitation to a 'hippy' life-style, though there is a kernel of evangelical truth in the hippy protest against the prevailing ethos. But it is certainly an invitation to be clear about the goals we set ourselves in human life and to recognize that the secondary goals, however important they may be, cannot bring us true rest, 'rest to our souls'. What we 'are' is more important than what we 'have'. 'Having' can never guarantee 'being'. To keep God in view – the sabbath of God to which the Fourth Commandment points us – also opens up the way to true freedom and rescues us from the fever of anxiety. A limit exists – not just the 'limit to growth' but a limit to our anxiety, a dimension which is not the result of our own provision and foresight but comes to us as a promise of rest, the rest which is anchored in God. The Sunday is the sign of this promise – the festival of freedom in a world of anxiety.

2. *The Ethos of Industriousness* is considered to be an attitude which is very much in keeping with the Bible and, above all, also a genuinely Reformed (and truly Swiss) approach to life. Nor can there be any objection to industriousness either on general human grounds or from a biblical standpoint. In the Wisdom literature of the Old Testament we already encounter the exhortation: 'Go to the ant, O sluggard; consider her ways and be wise. Without having any chief, officer or ruler, she prepares her food in summer, and gathers her sustenance in harvest . . . How long will you lie there, O sluggard? When will you arise from sleep? "A little sleep, a little slumber, a little folding of the hands to rest" and poverty will come upon you like a vagabond, and want like an armed man' (Prov.6:6-11). And in the eschatological perspective of the New Testament, there are very solemn exhortations to Christians to accept the obligation to be active in 'redeeming the time' by disciplined and responsible lives.

The questionable form of the 'ethos of industriousness' only comes on the scene when this approach is taken not just seriously but in such deadly earnest that it is idealized as the only way of life. This can happen not only to secular moralists (think, for example, of the hugely industrious rationalists of the Enlightenment who looked for the meaning of their lives solely in what could be used and rationally explained and considered everything incalculable and out of the ordinary as a waste of time!). But it can also lead religious people astray. H. G. Fritzsche cites the life-style of the revered pietist Spener as an illustration: 'He slept little but always well. He seldom dreamed and only twice in his life passed a night partly without sleep, and this, indeed, because of his concern for the Church. He rose regularly at five-thirty a.m. and on Sundays at four. He spent the whole morning until twelve noon and the first part of the afternoon receiving visitors. He permitted relaxation only at meal times and even this time was broken into by his habit of taking meals alone in his room on three evenings in the week. Indeed, so thrifty was he in his use of time that only twice in his entire life did he visit the garden behind his house in Berlin, and this for only a few minutes. On the other hand, to provide himself with exercise he would pace to and fro in his room during visits, and in addition to this, used his Sunday afternoon visits of inspection to rural parishes for the same purpose; but even on these and all his other journeys he had to have a book with him.'[37]

H. G. Fritzsche comments on this in the light of the Fourth Commandment 'Now it would be quite wrong to suggest that making Sunday afternoon visits of inspection was a clear breach of the Fourth Commandment. But from such a life style to real breaches of the commandments and not just of the fourth, could be only a short step. Especially when this life-style takes over in its secularized version and produces the typical managerial executive.'[38] The intellectual foundations are then laid in a 'secular asceticism' (as analyzed by Max Weber, for example) for modern capitalism, the industrious use of capital beyond all bounds. The sabbath may then be piously observed in religious circles but its gracious boundary, which is surely meant to bring benefits to the working day as well, to promote its ordering in freedom but not in a frenzy, is nevertheless transgressed. Industriousness then becomes something more than a secular aid to living and is turned into a secret – or avowed – goal of salvation.

3. *The Ethos of Success* is developed in close association with the two types of ethical thinking just outlined. In using this term 'the ethos of success' (or 'achievement') I refer to problems which are often discussed today under the rubric of a 'success or performance-oriented society' or the 'ideology of achievement'. These labels indicate the tendency of westerners today to define and seek the meaning and goal of their lives primarily in terms of work and 'know-how' (in the broadest sense of the word); to make the productiveness and usefulness

of their work the criterion of their value in relation to their fellow human beings. I said 'westerners' because this tendency has been more influential in 'Christian civilization' than in other cultural areas and because here it operates right across the frontiers between diverse social systems. While it is true that the worship of success has been developed and practised most widely in the capitalist system especially, the situation is not essentially any different in the socialist 'East'. To be sure, according to the 'plan', the rule there is that not 'performance' but human need is the focal point for the question of meaning and life in the coming communist society, but the fact is that, on the *way* to this goal, it is performance, productivity and efficacy which are the main requirements and in a very stringent degree.

This approach has ominous effects in both East and West. When the ideology of performance and the demand for performance prevail, it is mainly the less 'efficient' and the 'unproductive' who are affected. But even the successful ones, the achievers, are tempted to pursue a one-dimensional life-style in which the richness of human experience loses out. Here again, of course, we have to differentiate between 'success' and an 'ideology of success' or, to employ the terminology of the Reformation doctrine of justification, between 'works' and 'works righteousness'. We have no cause whatever to under-estimate success, work, economy, the productivity and fruits of the economic process, nor can we treat them with indifference. They represent an important element in our ordering of human life, both actively and passively, both in our own work and in our share in the work of our fellow human beings. This is expressly acknowledged in the Fourth Commandment when it refers explicitly to the right and duty of daily labour: 'six days shall you labour and do all your work'. We are not to reject as unbiblical the Reformed pietist view of work, namely, that it is part of our 'secular service of God'. But this attitude becomes more questionable when the productive output and success is elevated to the status of a proof of God's special grace and glorified as such, when work is regarded not just as our human right but also as our justification. When this happens meaning-ful achievement is replaced by an irrational ideology of achievement, meaningful work by an irrational works righte-ousness.

The Fourth Commandment prevents us from absolutizing our achievements and from the blindness and servitude to which this leads. And it does this in both variants of this temptation. In respect of the sabbath of God and of mankind, it recognizes in the initiative of the divine grace, i.e. in the reality which is beyond our reach and achievement and which is meant also to be reflected in our dealings with our fellow human beings in opposition to all forms of lovelessness in our relationships and social conditions, the ultimate basis and destiny of our human life. Understood in the way proposed in the Fourth Commandment, the Sunday, as the 'festival of freedom', signifies and fosters this central human concern: namely, the dimension of freedom in human existence which is never completely predictable, or, using the terminology of the author of the letter to the Hebrews: the sabbath rest of the people of God.

Authority and Reverence for Life

No Leap over the Wall!

In passing from the Fourth to the Fifth Commandment we
clearly cross the most evident boundary in the structure of the
Decalogue as a whole, namely, from the First to the Second
Table of the Law. It is important to assess the true significance
and status of this boundary. One possible misunderstanding
should be ruled out at once. There is no 'leap over the wall'
here. There is no wall dividing the two Tables. Theologically,
therefore, it would be disastrous to regard this crossing from
the First to the Second Table as a transition to a different order
of things (a *metabasis eis allo genos*). It would make little
difference whether we were to do so with a sigh of theological
regret at having to descend from the divine uplands into the
humiliations of the human, only too human, sphere, or with a
sense of relief at being clear, at last, of the religious clouds and
reaching the solid familiar ground of human life and social
relationships in all their earthiness.

To entertain such notions would only go to show that we
were posing unreal alternatives. Even here, God and humanity
cannot be divided; the ethic of the covenant presupposes the
indivisible unity of the two tables of the Decalogue. We were
able to watch this being demonstrated in detail in our exposition of the commandments of the First Table. These commandments of the First Table refused to stay up in the clouds,
in heaven; they link up directly with the patterns of human
behaviour in all areas of life and are not merely concerned with
cultic matters. We must expect the same thing in reverse in the
case of the commandments of the Second Table. Here, of
course, we shall be dealing with specific human relationships
and conditions, but not in any spuriously concrete way, as if

they could be considered theologically in and for themselves in abstraction from their context in the history of the Exodus, with no reference to the Preamble to the Decalogue with its vision and presentation of the divine name and promise.

The permeable nature of the boundary between the two tables of the Decalogue is very clearly illustrated in the Fifth Commandment. Its frame of reference is clearly indicated in the final clause: 'that your days may be long in the land which the Lord your God gives you'. Again, the first part of the commandment with its injunction to *'honour* your father and your mother . . .' points back to the First Table, where it was a question of really and truly honouring *God*. It is not surprising, therefore, that we find some uncertainty in the history of the interpretation of this Fifth Commandment as to whether it should really be counted in the First Table. I myself would not favour such a solution but we should certainly remember this hint that the Fifth Commandment represents, so to speak, a 'seam' in the Decalogue.

An Easy Commandment?

I would like to begin this interpretation of the Fifth Commandment with an autobiographical note. Years ago, when I was a young pastor in a Czech parish and had to preach for the first time on this commandment, I started with a rather categorical assertion: 'This is surely the easiest of all God's commandments'. Not that I would now wish to withdraw that statement. In 'ordinary, normal human experience' there is much to be said in its favour. If we think of the two human beings closest to us from the very beginning of our lives, the ones assigned to us, and if we think of all the more or less selfless devotion we experienced at their hands as children and even subsequently, we shall not find it very difficult to accept and obey this 'imperative' of the Decalogue: 'Honour your father and your mother . . .'. But I could not repeat the statement today and still assign it the same universal sense it had for me then. This is not because I have since learned that the old Rabbis took the very opposite view. They considered the Fifth Commandment to be the most difficult in the whole of the Law. The reasons for this were clearly economic since it imposed a lifelong burden on the 'breadwinners'. This burden can no longer be assessed as highly in our society but there are many other 'burdens' and problems which make it difficult if not impossible to talk of this commandment being the 'easiest'. Three points can be made here:

1. To honour father and mother never has been and never is 'easy' in a *completely universal* sense. I spoke just now of the 'normal' case, but in complex human relationships what is 'normal'? There have always been cases where children's lives, far from being enriched and encouraged by parents, are on the contrary disturbed and even ruined by them. Most of us could produce examples, from our own experience or from press reports, of cases where traumatic burdens have been imposed on human beings in this way throughout their childhood and adult life. Modern psychology and psychiatry have made our contemporaries far more aware of this than used to be the case. And while we must guard against ideological versions of such insights – I am thinking of the fashion of explaining human density in terms of a single cause or criminal acts in terms of childhood experiences – it is undoubtedly true that very real problems are being dealt with here.

2. In certain situations and *stages of development* it never has been and never is easy to maintain our relationship with parents intact, even in the 'best of cases'. There comes a time in almost all our lives when, as sons or daughters, we feel the need to keep our distance from our parents, a critical stage when we no longer accept unquestioningly the way proposed by them but scrutinize it critically or even reject it outright. This can lead to temporary and even permanent breaches, especially when parents react obstinately or tyrannically. The consequences of such breaches can be painful and even destructive, but they can also have an illuminating and cleansing role and mark a really positive advance along the road to maturity.

3. There are *periods in cultural history* in which the coexistence of the generations proves especially difficult. In the life of every society and civilization there are times when dissatisfaction with the traditional 'way of life' is felt with peculiar acuteness. These can be times not so much of public crisis as of an inner crisis of society, for example, in a period of relative prosperity, though a prosperity whose credibility has

become suspect. The 'achievements' of the older generation, instead of being taken for granted, are now seen in all their ambiguity and condemned on this score (especially when this older generation expects to be accepted as a matter of course). The established authorities come under attack, the parents in particular, as the ones closest to hand, but also in addition to them, the other representatives of the traditional order, the established 'father figures' and parental institutions – school, church, state and army. There no longer seem to be any really convincing reasons for continuing to honour father and mother. Many pointers today suggest that we are now living in just such a period characterised by a basic loss of confidence in established authorities.

For all these reasons, I am forced to the conclusion that (even) this Fifth Commandment can no longer count on general acceptance today. To regard it as a particularly 'easy' commandment would require us to turn a blind eye to the actual conditions in which we live today. The way of life to which this commandment points us is a narrow one. Yet, or just because of this, it is this way we must seek carefully and with discrimination in a theological ethic. Simply to abandon this commandment as archaic and old-fashioned on the grounds that our patterns of living are so radically different and so much more complex today would be a mistake. But it would also be a mistake to deplore the radical shifts and changes in the approach to this commandment and to hanker nostalgically for the 'normal healthy world' of the traditional patriarchal or matriarchal patterns. Theological ethics must avoid both these temptations. What this implies, I now wish to suggest in a fourfold argument.

Freedom as God's Creatures

At the beginning of the Second Table it will be best perhaps to start with a fundamental statement. The purpose of the divine commandments is to *order* the basic elements of *human life* as a whole; not simply its cultic and religious aspects but in all its social dimensions. *Coram Deo,* in the sight of God, the conditions and relationships of our social life are not trivial matters to which believers may turn a blind eye in an excess of piety and religious fervour, pleading 'superior' religious considerations, for example. On the contrary, they involve our relationship to God and, conversely, therefore, God and his message are concerned with them. The life of the family and with it, included in the family as its model, the whole wider circle of the human family and human society as a whole, emerge in consequence not as an amorphous or even chaotic realm but as an order established by God and to be ordered by humanity, and in this sense, an order *given in and with the creation.*

G. Ebeling comments as follows on this fundamental significance of the Fifth Commandment: 'When it comes to human relationships, the very first step is . . . so to speak an appeal to the basic experience of the divine presence within human society. The striking thing here in this Fifth Commandment is that it is not a prohibition, as in the case of all the following commandments. Nor is it a call to some specific act. What is required of us, one could say on the contrary, is something given in and with our life itself, the original causal connection of human coexistence. It is not something added on to human existence but lies at its very basis in the form of the union of man and woman with offspring in view. But it is certainly not the father-figure which is being emphasised here! What we should perceive, rather, is the primal force of human love from which human life is continually reproduced afresh: namely, this cooperation of humanity in the work of the Creator'.[39]

In Protestant theology (particularly Lutheran) the term 'orders of creation' has been employed to denote human social relationships in the field of marriage and the family. I am hesitant to use this term. If it is used, care must be taken not to use it uncritically. It is tempting to use it to describe not simply the covenant of fidelity between man and woman nor just the unique relationship between parents and children, but also a particular form of these relationships, as 'written into the creation'. The result is that certain culturally and historically determined structures tend to be regarded as fixed and absolute, as for example, a male-dominated marriage or a patriarchally structured nuclear family.

But no justification can be found for this in the divine commandment. The Bible does not imprison us in a timeless pattern of unalterable structures, fixed once and for all. On the contrary, it treats us as partners and allies in a history of liberation and salvation. It seems to me important here, at the beginning of the Second Table, to recall the setting of the Decalogue within the Exodus event, which I outlined and stressed in my introductory chapter. This also determines the direction our interpretation of the second half of the Decalogue must take: the commandments of the Second Table signify the deliverance of the people of God; they establish and accompany its freedom in relation to both God and humanity. Applied to the problems which arise in the area of the Fifth Commandment, this means that if a specific form of human life in society, in marriage and the family (and even in the wider community and society as a whole) contradicts the fundamental concern of the Decalogue with human liberation – if for example, one group, one sex, one generation is oppressed by another (and how often this is the case in the history of civilization and the Church) – then this structure can never be justified by appeal to the divine commandment. On the contrary, it must be changed.

But this change is no arbitrary anarchic one, no *creatio ex nihilo*. It takes place within a pattern established in creation. This is the positive significance of the otherwise ambivalent term 'orders of creation'. The freedom brought by the Exodus is a freedom which was prepared and foreordained from the very beginning, from the creation. And in respect of human life its very first word is: 'Honour your father and your mother!' I interpret this directive in the widest possible sense as a summons to be receptive to those who have preceded us in the creation and in history. This, surely, is the role of parents in our life. Biologically we derive from them. And in the ordinary way we owe our introduction into human community, culture and society to them. Our existence – and our freedom – is conditioned by this. Real human freedom is never simply a freedom to 'construct', to 'plan', to 'build', to 'rule'. Certainly to do these things is also a part of our freedom. The creation story itself records the mandate to humanity to rule the earth (*dominium terrae*) as a summons to freedom. But that is only one aspect of freedom. Freedom itself is distorted if the other aspect is not taken into account at the same time, namely, our origin and heritage, creation and history before us; in other words, recognition of that basic datum of our cohumanity to which Ebeling refers, namely, that community of love which is prior to each one of us, from which we derive, which we can only receive, can never 'make', produce, compel, or manipulate.

It is well known that Albert Schweitzer summed up his basic ethical concern in the phrase 'reverence for life'. This phrase is especially appropriate in the context of the Fifth Commandment. It corresponds to one vital aspect of the plea this commandment makes that we should 'honour' our father and our mother. In the light of this commandment, the realm of creation, the human beings and creatures surrounding us and helping to sustain us, acquire the status of supportive and protective values and the right to live in the sight of God and therefore in our sight, too. To desire to be free and yet at the same time to ignore and ride roughshod over this bond and the ethical obligation arising from it would be to misunderstand freedom and to replace it by a destructive and self-defeating arbitrariness. Today, faced as we are by the myriad ways in which our environment is being destroyed, perhaps we can the better learn to understand the timeliness and relevance of this Fifth Commandment.

The same critical awareness is also called for in respect of our historical origins, our cultural and social heritage. This 'family tree' also comes under the rubric of the Fifth Commandment. Here, too, we must ask what authority attaches to the tradition and community we enter at birth.

'Honour' — not 'worship'!

What specific conduct does the command 'Honour your father and your mother' require of us? First in relation to our parents, but then also in relation to our historical heritage? To avoid serious misunderstanding, the commandment is to be taken literally: we are *not* required to 'worship' our parents, if by worship we mean a compliance which excludes all further questioning. In modern terms, we are not required to indulge in any 'cult of personality', any glorification of established authority in the form of our 'elders', our 'superiors', our governments, nor even in any nostalgic or romantic apotheosis

of nature or history. Such interpretations have undeniably been
common in the history of the Church. The command 'honour
your father!' has been extended in the direction of patriarchy
(whereas a corresponding extension in the direction of
matriarchy, though it would have been just as or as little
justified, has for the most part never materialised). How often
have dignitaries of the church or of political life assumed a
formal role and behaved authoritatively as stern or friendly but
always 'superior' fathers. An authoritarian atmosphere has
thus been fostered in the family, the church and in government.
Nor was it only in Catholicism and Eastern Orthodoxy that this
happened but in Protestantism, too. I am thinking, for example, of certain trends in Lutheranism when support was given
to an authoritarian style of government which became wide-
spread in German territories especially, and even continued to
encumber political ethics there right down to our own times. (I
am thinking here of the controversies over Bishop Dibelius'
writings on 'government' in the sixties of this century, and of
the delight in episcopal and prelatical dignities in church circles.)

Such a onesided interpretation of the Fifth Commandment
fails to take sufficiently into account either the immediate or
the wider context. The biblical writers reject all such personality cults. This is quite clear from the Decalogue itself; consider
only the first two commandments! But the Fifth Commandment is controlled by the First. The Acts of the Apostles draws
the correct conclusion: 'We must obey God rather than men'
(Acts 5:29). This stimulates a critical questioning of every
proudly and arrogantly self-assertive authority in human
affairs. Moreover, the history of Jesus himself also points us in
this same direction. I am thinking of that remarkable scene
involving Jesus and his own family, when his mother and his
brothers try to arrest his activity (Mk.3:31ff.). There is a note
of severity in Jesus' answer: 'Who are my mother and my
brothers? . . . Whoever does the will of God is my brother and
sister and mother'.

In other words, certain interests in human life can be more
important than those of the family, the tradition, the supreme
earthly authorities. There are situations in which the tension
which results from this truth can only be resolved as we accept

painful conflicts. There are other extreme cases when the only course left is an 'Exodus' from the standardized patterns of the family, and of traditional ways of life and society. 'Dropping out' – in the forms in which whole groups of the younger generation have practised it in recent years in western countries – is a possibility. Older people should not automatically label and denounce this as a return to anarchy and chaos or as a breach with the orders of creation. Even on the basis of the Fifth Commandment, it can be legitimate to try the unconventional way. For this Commandment does not require us to glorify human beings, not even our nearest and dearest. What is required is not 'worship' of the family but, much more soberly, no more and no less that the 'honouring' of father and mother.

To understand more clearly the positive meaning of the word 'honour' we need to consider the original meaning of the Hebrew word so rendered. 'To honour' someone means to 'allow him or her due weight and importance', i.e. to take that person seriously, not wantonly to underestimate him or her. Another danger emerges here in our relationship to our predecessors and to the past: the temptation of the 'children' (in both the strict and wider senses), the temptation of the younger generation at a certain stage in their own development and experience of life, the temptation to simply ignore their elders, their parents; to think of them either in a kindly and condescending way simply as the 'old dears!' or else agressively and ruthlessly, in the belief that, as far as possible, a clean break with the past is needed.

Such an attitude is countered by the Fifth Commandment. Just because it forbids any glorification of the traditional authorities, just because it sets so much store by freedom, it also pleads the cause of freedom on the other side as well. The parents are to be honoured; they have their weight and importance and are not to be underestimated, devalued, in principle. We are to take seriously the views of the fathers and mothers, the historical heritage, even and especially when we refuse to take them 'in deadly earnest' but prefer rather to go our own way. The way of freedom is needlessly hampered from the very outset if we carve it out and pursue it ruthlessly over the bodies of our predecessors, when we turn it into a sectarian

programme entailing a 'complete' break with traditional
norms. The folly of such an attitude lies in its inhumanity, since
it ignores and despises the real human situation.

None of us starts life from zero. We always stand within
some historical context, in community with parents and even
grandparents. Without this tradition life would be impossible.
The wise thing is to accept this critically and deliberately; to
engage in dialogue with our elders, wrestling with the past
rather than choosing an uncritical flight from it. Certainly, on
the basis of this Fifth Commandment, the traditional patterns
cannot be given a blank cheque entitling them to unlimited
docility, but they *are* entitled to a credit loan of critical trust.
Their relative weight and importance, i.e. their dignity, is to be
respected. It is only by such an attitude to mothers and fathers,
at once dialogical and dialectical, that genuine freedom grows
in both church and society. If this balance is upset, either by
parents' manipulating children into a traditional posture of
submission or by the children's assumption that the parents are
automatically to be dismissed as unimportant, the real
'Exodus', the common liberation, is endangered. Honour your
father and your mother, therefore, as a matter of common
interest.

In this sense, therefore, the Fifth Commandment, which at
first sight seems to be concerned only with one group of human
beings, has a general significance, a dialectically inclusive scope
and purpose. It is dialectical also in the sense that the roles are
exchanged in the course of life. 'On the one hand, we are
always the ones addressed by this commandment; on the other
hand, we are also those named in the commandment. The
latter is no less crucial than the former. To whom do I owe
more? Those whom I myself should honour? Or those who,
because of me, find it difficult to honour father or mother? The
ones mentioned in the Commandment thus become those
addressed by it.' (Ebeling).[40] When the New Testament takes
up this Fifth Commandment in *Ephesians,* the apostle's exhortation is properly addressed to both sides: 'Children, obey your
parents in the Lord' and, equally, 'Parents, do not provoke
your children to wrath' (Eph.6:1 & 4).

The Increase of Life

One special feature of the Fifth Commandment must be noted. This commandment is not only anchored like all the others in the Exodus history, the event of liberation; it also includes an explicit statement of the goal of this history: '. . . that your days may be long in the land which the Lord your God gives you'. As is pointed out in the letter to the Ephesians, 'this is the first commandment with a promise' (Eph.6:2). This is a significant extra: the divine commandment is oriented towards the *promise*. This throws light on how we are to understand commandments, laws and ethical standards. For most people today, these terms are in bad odour. Those who are concerned to see a real change in existing conditions are especially suspicious of the phrase 'law and order'. And they have good cause to be suspicious of it. How often do powerful vested interests, even in the churches, barricade themselves behind this phrase. But it would be superficial and wrong to conclude from the misuse of this phrase that law and order are in themselves suspect and necessarily instruments of oppression.

Unless I am much mistaken, this prejudice plays a specially large part in the history of German culture, or at least a larger part than in the Anglo-Saxon or Czech tradition, and indeed, both on the right and the left in the debate. The theological task here is to bring out much more clearly the dimension of promise in the divine commandments and, by doing this, to unfreeze and set in movement again the entrenched positions on both sides. Two points will need to be emphasised: *(a)* ethical norms are rightly understood only when their dimension of promise is transparent. When they have been allowed to harden into a deadly legalism, they must be subjected to critical questioning and altered accordingly. But this change is *(b)* only to be endorsed and encouraged if it takes place not as a step in the direction of abolishing norms altogether and so into anarchy, but rather as an effort to approximate still more closely to the character of the commandments as a divine promise. Once more, the road to freedom lies between the temptations to legalism on the one hand and licence on the other.

But the Fifth Commandment goes further still. It spells out
the precise nature of the promise contained in the divine
commands: namely, the *'increase of life'*. From the standpoint
of the commandment, orderly relationships between children
and parents, indeed ordered social relationships of any kind,
are not ends in themselves. Their purpose is to protect and
increase life. Here is the justification of order and traditional
norms. Here is the basis of the authority of what has gone
before, but only here. They must be subjected to constructive
and critical scrutiny in the light of this criterion, this justification, i.e. in terms of their function in the service of life. There is
much talk today of the 'challenge to authority'. An anti-
authoritarian wave swept through most educational institutions
and societies in western countries around 1968, followed
shortly afterwards by a rather authoritarian reaction or
'backlash'. There were fierce clashes between opposing fac-
tions in families, schools and other institutions, including the
churches. Some light might have been thrown on this often
confused situation by an interpretation of the Fifth Commandment such as we have outlined. The all-important context
of real life is a safeguard here against turning the different
positions into ideologies. It is before this court, this superior
concern for the increase of life, for increased opportunities for
the afflicted to live, that we have to justify 'holding operations'
of every kind, as well as every challenging of established
positions.

Nor is the term 'life' to be left in the air unexplained here.
The Fifth Commandment speaks of 'the land which the Lord
your God gives you', i.e. the 'promised land'. This is certainly
intended quite concretely in the first instance, and refers to the
geographical goal of the Exodus. So too for us, the reference is
to quite concrete earthly circumstances. At the same time,
however, in the message of the prophets, the promised land
became a promise which transcends all earthly conditions, an
eschatological parable. These two references are inseparably
connected: the reference is to our earthly life but also to our
'new life' within this earthly life. To use the current jargon, it is
not just a question of quantity but also of the 'quality of life',
life as attested and defined in the New Testament with its
testimony to the way of life followed by Jesus of Nazareth. It is

therefore a question of renewing and deepening life's opportunities. What this means in actual practice is to be discovered in the Gospel of Jesus. Jesus himself summed it up most succinctly in his twofold commandment of love, the best commentary on which is his own liberating life. From the Christian standpoint, therefore, the deepest purpose of this Fifth Commandment and of all the divine commandments, is to guide and empower us to live in freedom and love.

The Imperative in the Norms

I began this commentary on the Fifth Commandment with a note concerning one fundamental principle, and I want to conclude it with another, this time, the *binding force of the commandments*. We all of us today feel the pressure of an almost universal change in ethical standards. Among Christians the result is a growing 'uncertainty'. In view of this rapid change, what still has any authority? To put it bluntly, are the Ten Commandments still binding on us? A Christian ethic must answer this question unequivocally. First of all, however, we need to know what a clear answer would mean. Would it consist in a legalistic 'Yes, of course, they are still binding'? Or in an antinomian 'Of course they are not!'? The Fifth Commandment in particular can help us to clear our minds here. It, too, contains a warning against false alternatives. It points in a different direction. From the standpoint of this commandment, the Ten Commandments retain their undiminished validity and authority as a clear declaration of the public will of God, at least for Christians and Jews, despite all the cultural changes. But this validity is not the validity of an abstract law; the commandments are valid in the living context in which they were set and given to us by God himself. In other words, as rooted in the history of the liberation of God's people and with the object of 'increasing' life in freedom and love. Within this life-giving context we must seek the concrete meaning of the Ten Commandments for the actual situation of our churches and congregations. This meaning is not something we already have or will ever have 'at our finger tips', firmly in our possession. God's commandment is never valid as a dead and deadening 'letter' but only as an imperative venture of freedom and love, the precise content of which must always be sought and practised in the given circumstances in which we find ourselves.

In this wrestling for certain knowledge of the will of God, we cannot let ourselves be tied automatically to our predecessors' theory and practice of the Ten Commandments. It will not be simply external pressures which prevent us from being tied in this way to traditional theory and practice, i.e. simply because of radical changes in the standards of the world, but above all, pressures from within, i.e. because the divine commandment itself calls us to fresh interpretations and new obedience in face of new dangers and new opportunities of love and freedom in our own times. Few of us, for example, would want to impose on society today the 'sabbath rest' as practised and imposed by law in Calvinistic Scotland in the 17th century. Many of us are urging a radical interpretation of the Sixth Commandment 'You shall not kill!' calling in question, as we do, the traditional doctrine of the 'just war' as advocated by our Reformation forbears; not simply by reference to the modern weapons of mass annihiliation, but also because of the Sermon on the Mount. Many are trying to disentangle the Seventh Commandment 'You shall not commit adultery!' from narrow and rigid interpretations and from a distrust of human sexuality, but not with any idea of suspending this commandment but rather in order to understand it as an encouragement to joyful fidelity and faithful joy. Here and elsewhere, therefore, we have to look for new ways and new norms. We are not at liberty to do so frivolously and arbitrarily. We shall honour the convictions of our fathers and mothers, but we shall do this, indeed, in accordance with the underlying meaning of the Fifth Commandment; namely, as grown-up sons and daughters and mindful of the fact that the 'great freedoms' of the Decalogue are greater than the interpretations given of them in the traditional norms.

You Shall Not Kill

The Archimedean Point of Ethics?

Even for non-church people, the Sixth Commandment seems the most *obvious* of all the commandments in the Decalogue. Bo Reicke comments on this with a faint note of wryness at the vagaries of the spirit of our times: 'Oddly enough, the prohibition of killing is the only part of the Decalogue now quoted as a rule of conduct in a secularized world'.[41] Ebeling takes a similar view: 'This is the only commandment in the Decalogue which can be taken up as a battle-cry even when a clean sweep has been made of all the rest in the interests of "emancipation"'.[42] The two theologians are drawing attention to a striking fact here: whereas there is a noticeable tendency in society and the church today to 'tone down' and 'relativize' most of the other commandments, we find theologians and political scientists increasingly applying the Sixth Commandment to ethical and political questions, above all, of course to the problem of war. And the consensus in this field seems to be growing in other respects, too. Whereas everything else in the ethical field seems to be in flux, it still seems to remain an unshakable axiom that people should not murder and kill. The categorical imperative of the Sixth Commandment seems to be a real 'Archimedean point' of ethics, whether Christian or secular.

But we must not oversimplify. Problems exist which cast doubt on the obviousness and authority even of this Sixth Commandment, and this, moreover, in respect of both the theory and the practice of this commandment. To begin with, even the *theoretical* basis of this commandment is not absolutely and completely clear. There is for example, the lexicographical fact that the Hebrew word used here (*'rasach'—'lo'tirsach*) is a relatively rare one in comparison

with other terms for 'killing'. It seems to denote a particular
kind of killing, particular in two senses: primarily the killing of
an individual enemy, the arbitrary act of depriving another of
life, an act of murder. It also denotes 'illegal killing, destructive
of community'. In other words, the word refers to acts whereby
the individual sets himself above the laws and in opposition to
the community. This, at any rate, is how it was understood in
the Old Testament. By this commandment the life of the
Israelite 'is protected against illegal and prohibited attack'.
'The Sixth Commandment thus takes its place in a community
which nevertheless had the death penalty and recognized war
as permissible and sometimes obligatory.' [43] In contrast to this,
the New Testament, the Sermon on the Mount (Mt.5:21ff.) in
particular, radicalizes the content and the range of this commandment.

Many difficult problems arise, in particular, in the *practical*
ethical (and political) context. Few of the commandments
confront us with as many and as painful a collection of
'borderline cases' as here. But by borderline cases are meant
situations in which the absolute validity and categorical force of
the commandment is 'limited', in greater or lesser degree
suspended. We need only mention one or two of these, such as
suicide, euthanasia, abortion, death penalty, war (to which we
shall have to come back in greater detail later), to realize how
much is still controversial even today in this field, indeed, that
today especially the validity of the Sixth Commandment is once
again in a state of flux in many respects. This does not make it
any the easier for theology today to interpret this commandment, however universally its validity may be recognized in
principle. We do not have even this commandment 'at our
finger tips', firmly in our grasp or clear in our minds.

A Commandment with Many Facets

This being the situation, it may be helpful to distinguish
between various aspects or levels of this commandment, without separating them. Let me first of all mention at least four
levels of the significance and scope of the Sixth Commandment.

1. The 'hard core' is relatively clear and unchallenged. Karl Barth sums it up in the following way (*Church Dogmatics* III/4, p.344). The commandment affirms that 'a human being may not be a murderer of a human being'. 'Human life is protected by this commandment . . . against arbitrary and therefore wicked extinction.' A directive of this kind speaks for itself. From both a human and a theological standpoint, *murder* is in every sense the last thing, the worst thing a human being can do to another human being. In murder we cross the ultimate boundary in relation to the fellow human being, i.e. by the irrevocable breach of this relationship, a breach which the perpetrator can never repair. Murder is the 'final solution' to the human conflict.

Theological reflection on this estimate of murder hardly seems to be necessary; human insight should suffice. But there are two reasons why we need to reflect theologically here. First, because the real sinfulness of murder can only be grasped theologically. Consciously or unconsciously, the murderer assumes the sovereignty over life and death and thereby claims the role which, from the biblical standpoint, belongs to the Creator alone. He (or she) 'plays God', in flagrant breach of the First Commandment, and in doing so usurps the right which has been bestowed by God on that fellow human being and which can therefore only be withdrawn by God himself, namely, the right to life itself. It is no accident that the reason given in Gen.9:6 for the protest against the shedding of blood in murder is simply: 'for God made man in his own image'. Above all here, where the ultimate is at stake, God and man belong together.

But it is not only in principle that the theological approach is important, but also in actual practice. This theological dimension sharpens and deepens the categorical rejection of murder. That murder represents the 'final solution' of human conflict and that it is therefore, from an ethical standpoint, really an 'impossible possibility' – this is something which everyone can understand. But how often in practice, and even in theory, this impossibility becomes a possibility and a reality close to hand. When the Bible presents murder and even fratricide as already beginning in the 'second' generation of the human family, with Cain and Abel (Gen.4), it is simply being realistic. The Bible is pointing out in this way that it is *possible* for the 'final possibility' to become not only the 'nearest possibility' in the world of human beings but even in fact the appalling reality. We human beings have always proved remarkably inventive in finding ways of obscuring this universally plain prohibition. The theological dimension of the divine commandment bars the way to any such clouding of the issue. I have no right arbitrarily to qualify and relativize this fundamental right of my fellow human being. The human right at stake here is in fact a God-given human right. In face of everything which could tempt us to settle conflicts by murder, therefore, the categorical imperative is 'You shall not kill!'

2. I mentioned the story of Cain and Abel just now. This story illustrates yet another aspect of the Sixth Commandment. It is the story of a murder but a story which is also interested in the subsequent *fate of the murderer,* pleading for his rights, rights which he has forfeited by his deed. According to Old Testament law, Cain deserves the death penalty for his murder of Abel. Henceforward he is subject to the appropriate judgement of his fellow human beings. Yet God takes even Cain under his protection to save him from the law of vengeance, however understandable that law may be. 'And the Lord put a mark on Cain, lest any who came upon him should kill him' (Gen.4:15). Here the second aspect or level of the Sixth Commandment appears. It opposes the 'law of the jungle', all strategies of unchecked destructive revenge. This is the vicious circle of sin, its inherent tendency to escalate. Here God steps in with his command. The Old Testament 'an eye for an eye, a tooth for a tooth' (Ex.21:14) sounds pitiless but, in its original context, it was itself an attempt to prevent killing from getting out of hand. Limits are established to the escalating tendency of vengeance. Even the murderer is not to be treated as an unprotected species, as 'fair game' for anyone to attack. Hence the mark on Cain's brow. Hence, too, the words of the Second Table of the Decalogue: 'You shall not kill!'

3. In the *New Testament* this line is continued and *radicalized* to a quite unexampled degree. For Christians the law of revenge is not simply limited but handed over to God: 'Beloved, never avenge yourselves, but leave it to the wrath of God, for it is written, "Vengeance is mine. I will repay, says the

Lord"' (Rom.12:19). But the most vivid and eloquent radical-
ization of the Sixth Commandment occurs in the teaching of
Jesus, in the passage in the Sermon on the Mount just referred
to: 'You have heard that it was said to the men of old, "You
shall not kill, and whoever kills shall be liable to judgement".
But I say to you that everyone who is angry with his brother
shall be liable to judgement' (Mt.5:21f.).

With these words Jesus 'de-restricts' the commandment, not
in order to make it so general as to weaken its force, but in
order to probe to the roots of murder. It is not enough to
prohibit murder, killing in the physical sense. It must never be
forgotten, of course, that this is the primary purpose of the
commandment. But there is an indissoluble link between the
outward deed and the inward thought. The outward eruption
of hostility, the physical blow, is very often no more that the
final explosion of a pent-up hatred, of a spontaneous or, far
worse, a nursed hatred for the fellow human being. In modern
jargon, there are 'structures' of murder in our human life, open
or concealed, and to take the Sixth Commandment seriously
also means uncovering and analyzing these structures and
counteracting them in time. Jesus' radical words, *'But I say to
you . . .'* encourage us to do just that. His motive here, of
course is not just sheer delight in being radical nor a mere
desire to shock the Pharisees. Nor is he propounding here a
'personalist ethic' of the exaggerated kind some have advocated. His concern, rather, is that we should be clear-sighted as
to the hidden strategies of murder and alert to its root causes –
intellectual, psychological and social – which operate on us and
influence our behaviour even beneath an outward show of
respectability. *Principiis obsta!* 'Nip the evil in the bud!' – this
is Jesus' contribution to the ethics of the Sixth Commandment.

4. The New Testament radicalizes the Sixth Commandment
not only intensively (i.e. by reaching down into the inner and
outward roots of sin) but also extensively as well. It is not
simply a matter of not killing, of refraining from murder, but
rather of taking positive action to *prevent* the threatened
destruction of life. The passage just cited from *Romans* about
vengeance spells this out when it continues: 'No, "if your
enemy is hungry, feed him; if he is thirsty, give him drink; for
by doing so you will heap burning coals upon his head"'

(Rom.12:20). The apostle then adds as a general directive: 'Do not be overcome of evil, but overcome evil with good' (12:21). The radical development of the Sixth Commandment in the Sermon on the Mount also points in this positive direction: reconciliation before it is too late; above all, an active willingness to reach agreement with our fellow human beings 'while we are still on the way (to court) with them' (Mt.5:25). It is particularly appropriate here, in reference to this Sixth Commandment, to link up with the supremely positive summary of the Second Table in the command to love our neighbours as ourselves: the deepest purpose of the prohibition: 'You shall not kill!' is to be found in the proffer of love, the practice of pro-existence, living *for* others.

I have been impressed by the clarity of the Reformers in seeing and developing this positive dynamic of the Sixth Commandment, the need to struggle against every 'murderous spirit' by taking both preventive and supportive measures. For example, in his brief exposition of the Sixth Commandment in the *Institutes,* Calvin emphasises our obligation, 'if we find anything of use in saving our neighbours' lives, faithfully to employ it: if there is anything that makes for their peace, to see to it; if anything harmful, to ward it off'.[45] And Luther has an even more vivid account of the matter in his *Large Catechism.* We are confronted with the command 'You shall not kill' not only where evil is being done but also whenever we fail to do the good we could, the good which is required of us: 'If, therefore, you send away one that is naked when you could clothe him, you have caused him to freeze to death; if you see one suffer hunger and do not give him food, you have caused him to starve. So also, if you see anyone innocently sentenced to death or in like distress, and do not save him, although you have ways and means to do so, you have killed him . . . for you have withheld your love from him and deprived him of the benefit whereby his life would have been saved'.[46]

These insights are particularly relevant today. In present conditions, of course, we also have to stress the social, political and structural aspects of these supportive measures. In an increasingly inter-dependent world, we are directly confronted with 'killing conditions' not only in our immediate but also in our remoter neighbourhood. On the basis of this Sixth Commandment especially, therefore, our practical obedience to the divine command must necessarily have a global dimension and also include a political concern, just as the ecumenical movement has tried to do in recent years in its programmes in the field of development, in the struggle against racism and in support of human rights. With this in mind, the 'Bread for our Neighbours' programme of the Swiss churches, the 'Christian Aid' programme in the United Kingdom, should therefore be energetically pursued in our congregations. Moreover, this is to be done not merely emotionally, idealistically, or in the form of sporadic philanthropic gestures but systematically and realistically in public action and efforts to create more just structures of neighbourly love. While the starting point of the Sixth Commandment is utterly concrete and personal, therefore, its interpretation and implementation nevertheless open up to us global horizons of social and ethical responsibility.

Summing up this attempt to grasp the core and the levels of the Sixth Commandment: the Bible begins with the very specific and sharp prohibition of Cain's murderous act; in doing so, however, it does not focus its gaze exclusively or with stupefaction on this admittedly final possibility and fact of human disobedience in the sight of God and of society, but goes on to probe and analyse it, to reflect, on its personal and social dimensions, and puts – to each one of us – the positive question: how the evil is to be overcome by commitment to the good at different levels.

We are not simply to equate all these stages and levels. There are distinctions in killing which are of great ethical importance. It would be wrong to relativize these distinctions as if they were 'degrees' of murder. At the same time, however, a Christian ethic has to elaborate and stress the real connections which exist between them, in order to keep awake the conscience of church and society. In the last analysis, killing means 'anything which diminishes a person's basic requirements for living, which cuts the ground from under the other person, even if this is done unintentionally, by sheer negligence, and not out of deliberate wickedness'.[47] It is not only Cain's sin of presumption which falls within the scope of the Sixth Commandment, but also the laziness and negligence of people like ourselves, our failures to respond to the need of our near and distant neighbours. The Sixth Commandment does not apply only to the extraordinary, exceptional areas of human life but to our ordinary everyday 'normality'. In the case of this commandment, too, we have to remember the total context of the Decalogue, the richly diverse history of the liberation of the people of God.

Borderline Cases of Killing: (1) Suicide

Against this background and within this total context we now turn to some of the borderline cases which are often discussed in ethical expositions of the Sixth Commandment. It would be impossible to mention all of them, still less to deal with them in a complete way with all their often extremely complex and controversial aspects. I select three of them to illustrate what has already been said.

I begin with *suicide* since here the killer's hand strikes the killer himself and not someone else. The deed remains, so to say, a 'private' matter. And this very 'privacy' can even be elevated to the status of a positive justification for the act of suicide. In some ancient philosophies, among the Stoics, for example, the deliberate choice of voluntary death by an individual was regarded as demonstrating the ultimate freedom available to the individual human being, the right to set a term to his life, not to let death take him by surprise, not to let dying become a punishment, his capacity, therefore, not only to live but also to die as a free person. *Exitus patet* (there is an exit available). Many people today, including Christians, find this deliberate termination of a person's own life at his own hands not altogether unreasonable. It is not all that long ago that the religious public in the USA were shaken by the suicide of a married couple of well-known theologians who, faced with the prospect of old age and sickness, a life with its possibilities exhausted, preferred to take this way out.

Suicide can take other forms, of course. I think of a friend in the Czech resistance. Broken by the agony of the tortures inflicted on him by the Gestapo during interrogation, he deliberately chose death not just to find release from his own sufferings but, above all, to rule out any possibility of his betraying the names of his comrades and to save his friends from falling into the hands of the Gestapo. Self-slaughter as self-sacrifice for the sake of others, therefore. The self-immolation of Jan Palach in Prague in 1969 illustrates another form of suicide. Palach intended his act as a deliberate 'witness to truth', an attempt to stir up his own church and society, to encourage his fellow-citizens to resist the dangers of lethargy, not to throw away the opportunities they still had of striving for liberation. Nor should we forget the Christian martyrs who actually invited their own death even if not themselves accomplishing it. Similar examples are found in the history of all peoples.

There is also, if the word may be forgiven, the 'normal' suicide: the flight from failure – or presumed failure – in life; the 'leap over the wall' out of some hopeless – or apparently hopeless – situation, in a mood of momentary depression, or even as an act of revenge directed against others. Suicide may take place as a violent reaction against some sudden crisis, unexpected or long feared. But it can also be the last step in a long almost imperceptible drift into a final act which apparently or really can no longer be postponed (and which is really a passion rather than an action).

In view of this very diversity of forms of suicide, it would be presumptuous to expect to find a sweeping dogmatic answer to the ethical problems of suicide. Christian theologians have often been guilty of such presumption in the past when they clothed their theological rejection of suicide in rigid legal forms and canon law. One example of this is the automatic refusal to allow those who have committed suicide to have a church burial or a final resting place in that portion of the cemetery reserved for those who have died 'normal' deaths. Efforts are being made today to avoid such sweeping judgements and even to take greater care with the terminology used. Suicide is distinguished from 'self-destruction' (i.e. between suicide as arbitrary and egotistic self-inflicted violence and 'self-destruction' as self-sacrifice). But even this is hardly satisfactory in view of the actual complexity of the circumstances in each particular case. From a theological and human standpoint, it would be much more to the point to achieve a more relaxed approach and to abandon the tendencies to legalism and casuistry in this area.

To dispel any misunderstanding here, this would not mean treating suicide in practice as a relative matter, as something quite 'normal', as an entirely open human possibility. Any such 'permissiveness' here is ruled out by the biblical command 'You shall not kill'. The purpose of the commandment is also to protect the life of the endangered person himself, against himself. If we believe in God as our Creator and Redeemer, we know that our own beginning and our own end are not within our own control or at our own disposal. The Christian must reject the ancient rule *'exitus patet'* (there is an exit) in favour of the biblical rule *'exodus patet'* (there is an exodus). The latter signifies that we have the promise of God's grace and faithfulness even (and perhaps especially) for 'hopeless situations'. Our human freedom is freedom for life, not for death. These are not two options equally open to us, not 'fifty-fifty' possibilities equally available to us and waiting on our decision. Despite everything, the Gospel is the 'Yes' – and not a 'Yes-No' – to life, our own life included, our own life especially.

But it is the *Gospel* and not the *Law* which utters this 'Yes'. The command 'You shall not kill' is certainly not to be understood as a call to hang on for grim life whatever the odds. We are to understand it concretely in the context of the Decalogue, of the history of liberation, by never losing sight of but always taking into account the 'attendant circumstances' and conditions which made this ultimately 'impossible' human decision possible. When this is done, there will be levels at which an act of deliberate self-sacrifice on behalf of others will certainly deserve respect. But above all, we shall adopt an attitude which refuses to deny the fellow human being the promise of grace, even when we disapprove or even condemn his act. Karl Barth has rightly said: 'If there is forgiveness of sins at all . . . there is surely forgiveness for suicide. The opinion that it alone is unforgivable rests on the false view that the last will and act of a human being in time, just because they are the last and take place, as it were, on the very threshold of eternity, are authoritatively and conclusively decisive for his eternal destiny and God's verdict on him. But this cannot be said of any isolated human will or act, and therefore not even of the last'.[48]

It follows from these two emphases that we are called 'to oppose unconditionally a threatened suicide (to refuse on principle to allow it), but also to recognize that a suicide which has in fact been committed has in some (in most) cases taken place just as much under grace as every other sin'.[49] The clearest ethical corollary to this attitude is the provision of a *preventive, prophylactic pastoral care* for people who are particularly at risk in this respect. This will also include preventive care in situations and circumstances which are 'potentially suicidal'. In the light of the Sixth Commandment, there is a vital and significant field of endeavour not only for personal and social ethics but also for pastoral care (including 'The Samaritan' telephone service).

(2) Abortion

My second illustration is abortion. Few ethical issues have been the subject of such passionate discussion and controversy in recent years in the 'Christian West' as this particular 'borderline case'. I say 'in the Christian West' advisedly, for the debate has flared up around the problem of the penal code of the *corpus christianum,* i.e. the question of the extent to which traditional moral theology of the church must be reflected in the penal laws of contemporary social systems. We are forced by the growing secularization of society to reexamine the logic of this and to do so, indeed, with a certain bias in favour of a liberalization of the law, a thesis made all the more attractive in view of the extreme severity which which abortion has been punished in some (though not in all) periods of church history. The pressure exerted by the liberalization lobby has, of course, provoked a counter-movement on the part of rather conservative-minded groups. The question posed by these groups is whether not only the church tradition but central values of western Christian humanism are not in danger here, in particular, the concern to protect defenceless human life threatened with extinction. Christians will certainly be in no doubt that this concern falls within the scope of the Sixth Commandment. The clash between contenders for these two positions has been especially vehement in most western countries.

In face of this stubborn and tangled situation, where an ideological dimension is deliberately added to the issue on both sides of the argument, we all need to make a special effort to remain sober and realistic. This also applies to those on the side of the church traditionalists, who, as I understand the matter, have a human concern to defend which is important both theologically and ethically. Moreover they have weightier arguments going for them here than they have in other social and ethical issues (in the traditional doctrine of war, for example). But it is a striking fact that, precisely on this question of abortion, they frantically declare a 'state of emergency', a 'crisis of faith' (which is certainly important enough but can not be regarded as the only such 'crisis'), a *status confessionis,* a situation which calls for a clear confession of the faith. Take the case of Bishop Lönning, for example. He resigned his episcopal position in protest against liberalising legislation in the Norwegian parliament on the issue of the interruption of pregnancies. However much we respect his sincerity, there is a real danger of turning this particular view of the question into an ideology. But the same danger is no less evident on the other side, too. Militant liberalizing groups often attach such importance to this issue that it would seem that freedom today is equated with the freedom to abort. Even socialists often become pure liberalisers on this issue, i.e. defenders of an abstract individualistic view of freedom. Slogans such as 'my body is mine', on the one side, or the crude and provocative assertion that 'abortion is murder', on the other side, do very little to promote ethical clarity or mutual understanding.

As I see it, against this unhappy background of divergent dogmatically rigid positions and in the light of the Decalogue, the attitude of theological ethics should be both open-ended and committed. By 'committed', I mean aware of the binding connection between this ethical problem and the Sixth Commandment, 'You shall not kill'. This connection is often denied. It is argued, for example, that the foetus is not really a human being but only a *portio mulieris* (part of the woman) or a *pars viscerum matris* (part of the mother's womb), as Roman law and Stoic philosophy asserted. It is true that the embryo is not really a human being, i.e. not a fully-developed human being. But the other statement must be challenged. The foetus is, from the standpoint of both structure and density, 'a being on the way to human being' (as H. Saner neatly puts it in a valuable account of the problem).[50] Biology and theology are in agreement here, therefore. What is involved in the termination of a pregnancy is an interception of the process of human development, indeed, the development of a human being, an intervention against the 'neighbour' (here in the most literal sense the 'neighbour'). 'Even what has still to become a human being is *already* a human being' (Tertullian). From the biblical standpoint, the still unborn creature is undoubtedly also entitled to the protection of the Sixth Commandment *and* the concern of love. Here too, real freedom is freedom in pro-existence. Under no circumstances can Christian theology fail to make this binding reference.

It should do so, however, with a relaxed and *open* outlook. In other words, here too we must reject all forms of crude dogmatism and legalism. Let me remind you of what I said earlier by way of introduction about the different levels of the Sixth Commandment. This calls for application here. The question of abortion falls within the scope of the Sixth Commandment. But the command 'You shall not kill' is a directive which must be discovered anew in different situations; it is not a blanket prohibition, not a sweeping generalisation. The slogan 'abortion is murder' is just as much an over-simplification as the slogan 'my body is mine'.

There are different stages in killing. This is particularly true in the case of abortion. From the standpoint of the purpose of the divine commandment, it is highly suspect not to say downright hypocritical to single out the last visible stage in the whole connected series of conflict situations, i.e. the act of the pregnant woman, and then to concentrate the moral sanctions (not to mention the penal sanctions) exclusively on this final act. What theological ethics needs to urge here is the radical extension of the commandment along the lines of the New Testament. In other words, we must show greater understanding for the personal and social causes of the conflicts to which the neighbour is exposed in this area. In debates on this issue, much attention has already been given to the importance of 'supportive' and 'preventive' measures and pastoral care, here especially, and, above all, to the need for sexual education and social and political measures to help people in such difficulties. It is at this prophylactic level particularly, not just at the level of penal law, that the Church and theologians should be engaged.

Just a word on the term 'penal law'. It may well be questioned whether it is right to couple the ethical problems here with the criminal code. There is much to be said for Hans Saner's view in the conclusion of his essay: 'The interruption of pregnancy really has no place in the criminal code'.[51] At any rate, churches and theologians must be realistic enough to recognize that, with the disintegration of the 'Christian West', their tradition is no longer going to be automatically reflected in criminal law. To the extent that this is a threat to important values, they will have substantial grounds for deploring it. But they must not shut out this possibility on principle. They have never been promised the 'privilege' of living to the end of time in the conditions of a 'Constantinian society' (nor the necessity of doing so). There will always be times, even in the West, when the Church will only be able to commend its ethic by using its own resources – preaching, pastoral care, the instruction of its own members. There will be losses and gains here. Gains, because there will be new opportunities of witnessing in a committed and open way, without institutionalized nostalgia or vested interests. The experience of Christians in Eastern Europe has shown that such a situation need not necessarily damage the credibility of the Christian life even in the ethical field.

Meanwhile, things have not yet reached that pass. In western countries the Church still has an 'official' position in society. It cannot shrug off its responsibilities for the reform and development of the penal code. The reform of the laws governing pregnancy is also its concern, therefore. It can and should make its views known.

But in which direction? This is a relatively open question in the Protestant churches. Some churches, including the Swiss Protestant Federation, have made important statements on the issue. Not to dodge giving a personal opinion here, I would want to say that, in the present situation (and therefore without any dogmatic inflexibility, therefore), relatively the most sensible option would be to emphasise the *broader indications*. By 'broader' I do not mean simply to urge that due consideration be given to the eugenic, medical, legal and, in real cases of conflict and distress, the social factors involved, but also that social responsibility should be widened to include the 'supportive measures' mentioned earlier, with special concentration on the consideration of the position of the underprivileged in church and society. This option, it seems to me, closely matches the concern for 'commitment' and 'openness' which I emphasised in reference to the current debates. But I regard as less acceptable the law legalizing abortion within three months of conception. For two reasons: firstly, because it 'allows a certain period in which those already born have an absolute right to dispose of the as-yet unborn . . . and this once again is open to question', as even H. Saner, who favours this solution, rightly acknowledges.[52] The second reason is that, by giving unqualified permission to intervene within a very arbitrarily determined period of time, this solution gives the impression that the termination of a pregnancy within this period is somehow 'normalised' and therefore becomes a quasi-normal procedure, which, in the light of the Sixth Commandment, it certainly is not.

War as a Borderline Case?

My third example of a borderline case is a manifestly *social and political* one: namely, the *problem of war*. Some will argue that this problem lies outside the scope of the Sixth Commandment, since war is not only conducted but even legitimized within the very shadow of the Old Testament Decalogue. At any rate this factor of human history is seldom opposed in the Old Testament with any reference to the Sixth Commandment. The facts are hardly in dispute. Even within the shadow of the Decalogue, the ancient people of God could be extremely warlike in their conduct. The prohibition of killing obviously applied primarily to the wilful act of the individual; there is no similar denouncement in so many words of the political act of killing in war. But even in the Old Testament we find a growing disquiet about war in the messages of the prophets and a concentration on *shalom* (peace) in both the personal and the social sense. For the covenant people, therefore, the ultimate promise of the new covenant means peace and life, not sword and slaughter. It is indeed along these lines that the 'new covenant' is understood in the history of Jesus Christ. Christ's sovereignty is not one which makes use of political power to dominate and oppress people but uses rather the power of love which is politically powerless. The *magna carta* of this sovereignty is the Sermon on the Mount. And in this sermon, the Sixth Commandment in particular is interpreted as a summons to strive for reconciliation with the enemy, the establishment of peace, historically and eschatologically.

Throughout most of church history, especially after Constantine when Christianity acquired the status of a 'state religion', the old view of the commandment rather than the new became the established approach. For centuries Christian ethical experts and theologians sought to 'canonize' war. By this ambiguous term we mean the thoroughly serious ethical task of keeping this monstrous phenomenon of war within bounds, both theologically and politically. In our sinful world war is a brutal fact. We know this both from the Bible and from our own historical experience. It is impossible for the Church simply to ignore this fact; the least it can do is to keep war in check and to try to humanize it. In both the realm of theory and of practice, a good deal of energy has been applied in the endeavour to do this throughout church history.

The classic form of this effort, theologically, was the doctrine of the 'just war' *(bellum iustum)*. Christians can only take part in war if certain conditions are fulfilled. These criteria of a just war are summed up largely in five points: 1. the cause must be just *(causa iusta)*; war is a last resort in the effort to restore a justice which has been violated; 2. it must have a *recta intentio*; the goal of war is peace *(pax)*, common life with, and therefore not the destruction of, the enemy; 3. the means must be appropriate *(debitus modus)*; only morally defensible methods of warfare are permissible; the 'rules of war' must be respected; 4. war must be conducted only by the lawful government *(legitima potestas)*; 5. the goods involved must be weighed; the benefits of war outweigh the damage it inflicts.

It is impossible to deny the *recta intentio* of this theory, defended by both Catholic and Protestant theologians, or its actual influence in the direction of humanizing warfare. Yet there were certain drawbacks attached to it. As a theory, it not only curbed war but also dulled the cutting edge and influence of the biblical message ethically and socially. In particular, it blunted the radical interpretation of the Sixth Commandment in the Sermon on the Mount by being too ready to accommodate the command 'You shall not kill' to the pattern of this world. It led all too easily in practice to the legitimizing of extremely ambiguous political power struggles (there was scarcely a single war in the history of the West which did not declare itself a 'just war'). Above all, however, the traditional doctrine of the just war 'canonized' war itself (in the other utterly dubious sense of the term) by pronouncing it a quite defensible Christian way of settling human conflicts. Under cover of this latter pronouncement, it became possible to 'glorify' war and to practise it enthusiastically right down to our own times, in the First World War (for example, in the German theology in the modern period).[53]

Only after the Second World War was there a far-reaching change in ecumenical social ethics. This took place mainly under pressures from outside, as a result of the lessons learned from the observation of the incalculably intensified destructive power of modern weapons, rather than as a result of theological reflection. The fact is that, following Hiroshima and Nagasaki, after the further development of weapons of mass destruction of all kinds in recent decades, the traditional doctrine of war loses all touch with the realities of modern warfare. The concept of war as the 'continuation of policy by other means' (Clausewitz) can scarcely be used any more. With the new technological weapons, the total destruction, the extinction of all human life on earth becomes a real possibly. Today, therefore, 'war as we have known it for 6,000 years has finally become antiquated' (C. F. von Weizsäcker).

This change obviously has implications for the theological view of war. Just think of all those patiently wrought theories of the conditions for a 'just war'. Not one of them remains untouched and invulnerable. There is *no* justice which could be restored by a nuclear war. After such a nuclear war there is no shared co-existence with an enemy, but only a shared 'non-existence'. Given weapons of mass destruction, there are no longer any legitimate 'instruments of warfare' or 'rules of war'. There is no legitimate authority which could act as the military agent to strike such a blow against the whole human race. Nor is there any benefit or value which could be deemed to outweigh the damages inflicted by nuclear war. From the ethical standpoint, therefore, war becomes increasingly the 'anti-instrument', the 'non-instrument' of policy today; in the case of war fought with nuclear weapons, unqualifiedly so, but even in the case of war fought with 'conventional' weapons, in view of the dangers of escalation. War, therefore, is no longer a Christian option.

It is here, in the light of these new experiences that theological ethics has been and continues to be challenged to re-examine its heritage and mission, and to do so both critically, in respect for example of the above-mentioned revision of the doctrine of the 'just war', and also positively. Here the question of the scope of the Sixth Commandment could play an important role. The record of theology in this matter is not entirely clean. But there is at least one tradition which it could reflect on, a tradition which for the most part has been harrassed and suppressed by the official Church but which has nevertheless been present and active right throughout church history, namely, the *pacificist tradition*. In this tradition, in the witness of the historic peace churches and of nonconformist pioneers (such as the Czech Hussite, Petr Chelcicky in the period of the Reformation, and Martin Luther King in our own lifetime), the commandment 'You shall not kill' was unhesitatingly applied to the social and political sphere and there translated into a challenge to a radical and concrete effort for peace, appealing to the example and the resurrection of Jesus.

In my view, this tradition needs to be reexamined today, critically but with an open mind. Critically, so as to avoid the political passivity and legalism which have sometimes hampered the pacifist witness in the past; but openly and receptively, too, emphasising that under the sovereignty of Christ it is impossible to exclude certain areas of life *a priori* from the binding force of the Sixth Commandment. The command 'You shall not kill' also points the way for us as Christians in the political field, not as an automatic recipe and law but certainly – and thoroughly in harmony with the intention of the Decalogue – as a stimulus and encouragement to us to show the required commitment in this field. In the immediate context, this means showing persistence and inventiveness both in the study of the whole question of peace and in work for peace, and working together and with others in the prevention of human slaughter at every level of our common life.

You Shall Not Commit Adultery

The Debris of Church History

From the standpoint of current morality, the exposed position
of this commandment in the Second Table of the Decalogue
and the corresponding importance thus attached to it seem
puzzling and even rather offensive. The prohibition of adultery
stands between the prohibition of killing and the prohibition of
theft, these latter prohibitions being the two which are still
treated fairly seriously in contemporary morality and jurisprudence even today. Their validity is still recognized in principle
and even in the details of the criminal code. The same cannot
be said of the Seventh Commandment, which therefore
appears to be the odd man out.

In most countries, the civil laws of marriage and divorce have
been liberalised and, in the prevailing ethical climate, divorce
has almost entirely ceased to be regarded as a punishable
offence; if any blame attaches to it at all, it is only as no more
than a trivial offence, a mere peccadillo. In some rarefied
circles, indeed, you are only in the fashion if you treat yourself
to a divorce from time to time. The fact that, in the Old
Testament, adultery, like murder, was punishable by death can
only be regarded by most people as a relic of barbaric times.
But quite apart from the appalling severity exercised in the
enforcement of the Seventh Commandment (although this is
revised in the Bible itself, as Jn.8:1-11 reminds us by recording
the strong protest of Jesus himself against those who condemned the woman taken in adultery), the close association of
the commandment with those on either side of it is itself felt to
be offensive.

In theological ethics it is important to keep in view this
widening gap between the Seventh Commandment and current

theory and practice. But we must do so carefully, and that means, self-critically; not rushing to attack and overwhelm it by polemical broadsides condemning the 'decadence' and 'permissiveness' of our civilization. The mutual estrangement here is not to be attributed exclusively to the secular morality of our time. The Church must accept its share of the blame. The history of the interpretation of the Seventh Commandment is far from having been a glorious chapter in the history of Christian or Jewish ethics. H. J. Kraus rightly points out: 'Since earliest times, the interpretation of the commandment "You shall not commit adultery" has carried along with it in the stream of tradition the debris of culturally conditioned ideas and concepts which to some extent already silted over the true intention of the biblical directives on marriage'.[54] He goes on to refer to two attitudes which are still influential today. *First,* the idea of marriage as a 'property relationship in which the husband is the owner (Heb. *baal*) who rules and decides'; in other words, the patriarchal distortion of the Seventh Commandment and the double standard by which judgements are accordingly regulated. Whereas the husband could only break up someone else's marriage, the wife was also made the chief culprit for the breakdown of her own. *Secondly,* the idea of marriage as a 'tabu sexual zone in which the laws of discipline and order prevail', an attitude made possible, above all, by an unbiblical hostility to sex which was also operative in church history (especially in the medieval period). A *third* attitude could also be added here, usually in combination with the first two, namely, a strong tendency to adopt an attitude of moralistic and legalistic strictness, especially in respect of the Seventh Commandment. Pharisaic self-righteousness tends to take special delight in dwelling on and sounding off about sexual and marital offences. Far too little attention has generally been paid in the theory and practice of the Church to the liberating example of Jesus in the pericope from the Fourth Gospel, to which reference was made earlier.

A good deal of leeway has to be made up in church ethics if the Seventh Commandment is to be presented credibly in both theory and practice. There is a good deal of 'debris' and 'silt' from cultural and theological history to be cleared out of the way. That having been said, however, we can and must still stand by the Seventh Commandment, and with the same firmness and commitment as in the case of all the rest, not least the one which precedes it and the one which follows.

What is at stake in this commandment? Why is it so important? In the following attempt to answer these questions, I want to proceed in two stages, constituting as it were two concentric circles, and to consider the command both in its narrower and in its broader sense. Primarily and centrally, of course, the command focusses on a specific human relationship, that of marriage. In the German, the commandment is literally: 'You shall not break up a marriage *(ehebrechen)'*. But translations in other languages interpret the commandment in a broader sense (as e.g. the Czech *neselmilnis*), covering the whole range of man-woman relationships, not only in marriage but in every other respect as well. Such an interpretation goes beyond the immediate sense of the biblical words but it is by no means an arbitrary one. Within the broad context of anthropology and salvation history in the Old Testament, marriage is already a paradigm of complete human fellowship and an image of the true covenant between God and his people. And in the Sermon on the Mount, a key New Testament passage for our understanding of this commandment, the scope of the commandment is radically developed to take in not just the breach of a particular marriage covenant by an act of marital infidelity but also every movement tending in this direction, all unfaithful conduct and thought in respect of the fellow human being of the opposite sex (Mt.5:27ff.).

The Man-Woman Relationship: The Basic Form of Co-Humanity

I want to begin with this broader interpretation because, by doing so, the key role of the Seventh Commandment within the Decalogue as a whole – immediately following the prohibition of murder – will perhaps become clearer. What the Seventh Commandment is concerned with is not just minor details of our private conduct but the basic dimension of our human existence, our co-humanity. For the man-woman relationship is *the basic form of co-humanity,* of human society, human solidarity. Just consider the two accounts of creation in the Old Testament. In many respects they are dissimilar yet both agree in recognizing that God's human creature is essentially a co-human being. In the second account of creation, for example, Adam appears at first in the new created world without any human counterpart but has immediately to learn that 'it is not good that the human being should be alone' (Gen.2:18). And this truth is stated at a higher level of theological reflection in the first account of creation by a fundamental affirmation of the biblical view of humanity; 'And God created humankind in his own image, in the image of God he created humankind; male and female he created them' (Gen.1:27). In a *single* 'divine breath', the likeness of humankind to God *and* the co-human character of our humanity are established. Humankind, the human being, is not self-contained but is constituted and develops in relationship to God and to the fellow human being. Without the fellow human being, the human being is not complete but, as Karl Barth puts it, 'a ghost of a human being'.

But the basic concept of co-humanity is not presented in the two accounts of creation merely in general terms. A specific culminating point is emphasised, namely, the co-humanity of *man and woman*. For Adam, Eve represents the irreplaceable and helpful 'thou', and *vice versa*. The concrete form of the co-humanity of the human creature made in God's image is the co-humanity of man and woman, woman and man. We must reflect on the theological significance of this view of humanity. What is the doctrinal and ethical significance of the fact that, in the very first biblical statements about our human existence, this specific dialectic of co-humanity is given such prominence?

Few theologians have examined this matter as thoroughly and in as much detail as Karl Barth has done in the anthropological volumes of his *Church Dogmatics*. The conclusion he comes to is quite unambiguous, perhaps one-sided: 'The human being never exists simply as a human being but always as a male or female human being'.[55] There are many forms of co-humanity. We are privileged and obliged to live in relationship in a variety of contexts. Influences from many different quarters go to shape our personal life. There are relationships between races, classes, cultures, religions; we are marked by relations between the generations and by predispositions of character. All these relationships and influences leave their deep mark on our character. Anthropologically speaking, however, the man-woman relationship is incomparable. 'A human being is necessarily and totally man *or* woman and, as such and in consequence, just as necessarily and totally man *and* woman. We can neither wish to emancipate ourselves from the *differentiation* and to live simply as "human beings" transcending our given male or female condition . . . nor can we wish to emancipate ourselves from the *relationship* and thus to be simply the man without the woman or the woman without the man.' [56] The man-woman relationship is the basic model of the co-humanity intended at the creation.

It is with this essential realm of life that the Seventh Commandment in its broader sense deals. Its key position within the Decalogue now makes more sense: the ethical relevance of this vitally important realm matches the anthropological importance of this man-woman relationship. Pushing it a bit, we could say that it is not altogether arbitrary that this commandment should follow hard on the heels of the prohibition of murder. Precisely here, in our relationship with the 'opposite sex', we can let human life down completely – that of our fellow human beings and our own – and in this sense, or even literally, 'destroy' it. The man-woman relationship becomes *the acid test of our humanity*.

The reflections of the young Karl Marx on this theme are astonishingly clear and sharp-sighted. Even if we start from different presuppositions and have a completely different context of thought, we do well to attend carefully to what he has to say: 'The immediate, natural, necessary relations of person to person is the *relationship of man to woman*. In this *natural* species-relationship, the relation of the human being to nature is immediately to the fellow human being . . . . It is possible to judge from this relationship the entire level of development of humanity . . . This relationship also demonstrates the extent to which the human being's *needs* have become *human* needs, hence the extent to which the *other,* as a human being, has become a personal need, the extent to which, in existence at its most personal, the human individual is at the same time a communal being'.[57]

Within the perspective of the Decalogue, what does it signify to think of this relationship as an 'acid test of humanity'?

Reflection on the historical context of the Ten Commandments seems to me to be important and helpful in any attempt to give a theological answer to this question. As we have insisted, the Decalogue is the document of a deliverance and a covenant, a 'signpost to freedom' directly connected with the establishment of the covenant. These two concepts, 'freedom' and 'covenant', are vital for any understanding of the Seventh Commandment. The command 'You shall not commit adultery' is not simply a disciplinary legal measure in the area of human sexuality. If we approach the commandment from this angle, and it is notorious that there have been many such approaches in the history of the exegesis of this commandment, we miss its whole point. There can be no going back on what has already been said, of course. The man-woman relationship is the dimension of the human which was assigned it at the creation and is fundamentally good, therefore. We have to reflect on it, develop it, indeed cultivate it. Hostility to eros and hatred of sex are not Christian virtues. Any tabu on sexuality in the practical implementation of this commandment is out of place. Rather we are required to maintain and demonstrate freedom in this essential area of life.

But this is just the question. What precisely do we mean here by freedom? In the context of the Ten Commandments, of course, this freedom must be understood in the light of the covenant, along the line indicated by the biblical covenant as an event. It is impressive how often in the Bible the man-woman relationship is considered in close proximity to the covenant relation between Yahweh and his people (cf. Hosea 2:16ff.20ff; 3:1ff.) On the debit side: the recurring experience of Israel in its inevitable contacts with the free-wheeling religious sexuality of the near-East fertility cults all around it was that chaotic sexuality often goes hand in hand with a chaotic religiosity, infidelity to God with infidelity to the fellow human being. On the credit side: Israel experienced Yahweh's fidelity to the covenant and this was a constant spur to and encouragement of fidelity in human relationships. The keynotes of the freedom in view here are solidarity, fidelity and commitment.

Understood in this way, the signpost to freedom established in the Seventh Commandment is, as I see it, still valid today and perhaps even more *relevant* than ever. In the theory and practice of sexual ethics, a far reaching change has been taking place before our very eyes in recent times. Increasingly reliable contraceptive devices have removed a whole series of risks from sexual practice. Many tabus have been almost completely abandoned in education and culture. We find exponents of the 'new morality' proclaiming that the spontaneous expression of uninhibited sexuality will gradually inaugurate a general improvement of human life and society. People live and think today with a new 'freedom' – in some cases though not in all, they are doing so with all the enthusiasm of committed freedom fighters. This provokes the opposition of those to whom this kaleidoscopically 'permissive' scene assumes almost apocalyptic dimensions.

The Seventh Commandment requires of us a more discriminating and realistic attitude. It does not insist that we reject out of hand the changes taking place in contemporary sexual morality. The fact is that important aspects of human liberation are linked with these changes. The abandonment of narrow moralistic puritanical attitudes to sexuality and of the misguided tabus which littered this aspect of life under the guise of 'Christian morality' is to be welcomed. And welcomed, not least, from a biblical standpoint too, in view of the natural, straightforward and spontaneous way in which the Old Testament is able to celebrate love between man and woman. At the same time, it must also be emphasised here that, from the biblical standpoint, this spontaneity and freedom do not mean any absence of commitment and obligation. Genuine liberation achieves its goal in human relationships only when there is fidelity, a fidelity which is *voluntary and free,* of course, not one which is externally imposed and legally enforced. Yet a free *fidelity,* i.e. a realistic recognition that freedom in relation to the neighbour (and to God) does not mean permissive experimentation (even if in other contexts this may be a legitimate exercise of freedom) but the demonstration of fidelity. On the basis of the Seventh Commandment and of the whole Decalogue, it is the 'covenant of freedom' which gives the direction for the man-woman relationship.

The Shared Life of Marriage

This brings us to the question of the shared life of marriage and so to the consideration of the commandment 'You shall not

commit adultery' in its more restricted sense. I am not speaking
of marriage as an institution but of the 'life covenant', the
'shared life' of marriage. Normally, of course, marriage does
have an institutional aspect, determined by culture and custom,
and rightly so, since marriage is not just a private union but an
open and public one, too. Yet marriage in the sense of the
Seventh Commandment is not simply to be equated with any
particular institutional form. One good reason why not is
already provided by the extremely diverse and changing view
and practice of marriage as an institution in the Old Testament
itself. The fundamental trend within Israel is certainly in the
direction of marriage as the lifelong monogamous union of one
man   and   one   woman.   This   trend   is   also   influenced,
undoubtedly, by the idea of the covenant and, from the Christian standpoint, the 'monogamous marriage' is certainly the
possibility we are committed to strive for according to the New
Testament. But it is sensible to distinguish between 'marriage'
and its 'forms'. Marriage is essentially a community of life,
whose form is constantly to be renewed.

My reason for emphasising this is to guard against a possible
misunderstanding. Marriage has a relatively 'bad press' today,
especially among young people. Marriage comes under heavy
fire in the process of change referred to earlier. In society today
there is a strong current of opinion which rejects the legalized
'entry into the married state', and, in some cases, for reasons
which deserve respect, in the sense of a protest against a
'patriarchal', 'bourgeois', 'hypocritical' institution. These three
adjectives point to factors which can hamper and even destroy
the community of love and life. They have connections with the
traditional institution of marriage in the culture and society of a
particular juncture, in our case, that of late-capitalism. To
protest against these things, for example, against a family law
and a family morality which discriminates against the woman,
is possible and even long overdue. The refusal to accept these
structures too readily can certainly be a responsible attitude.
But despite the disintegration of many of the traditional forms
of marriage as an institution, the community of life between
man and woman is in no way invalidated. Despite all the ways
in which marriage in this sense has been distorted and
straitjacketed in history, it remains a way of life established at

the creation for the man-woman relationship and still well-worth striving for and developing, for all the ambiguities of its history.

To avoid any misunderstanding of this vote of confidence in marriage, let me at once point out that marriage is *not the only* form the man-woman relationship can take, still less the only commanded form. Tendencies in this direction can be found in the Protestant ethic (as in the Jewish ethic before it). Marriage has even been regarded here sometimes as the first duty of Christians. Even in our own time we can still find a statement like the following from Paul Althaus: 'Marriage is the instrument for the procreation of new life. No one has the right to evade the will of God the Creator who, through the human constitution and the pressures of nature, commands us to multiply. And marriage is the supreme task of personal community which no one has the right to evade'.[58] There are a number of problems in such an approach. There is the extremely questionable way in which it subordinates marriage to the procreative instinct; it almost reminds us of the slogan: 'The first duty of citizens is to beget children'. It also involves a questionable narrowing of perspective by the emphasis on the aspect of 'law'. It fails to do justice to the character of marriage as a free covenant. Above all, it is discriminatory in principle, branding the *unmarried* as 'disobedient' or abnormal people, a value judgement for which there is no support whatever in the Bible. The fact that, at the very centre of the New Testament, we find an unmarried person presented as 'true man' speaks for itself. The temptation to 'matrimonialize' the co-humanity of man and woman must be resisted therefore, subject only to the qualification that marriage is and remains the paradigm and test case for this relationship. The fact that the only commandment addressed directly to this set of problems is formulated in this way – 'You shall not commit *adultery*' – points unmistakably in this direction.

What is marriage then? I adopt Karl Barth's definition: it is 'the form of the encounter of man and woman in which the free mutual harmonious choice of love on the part of a particular man and a particular woman leads to a responsibly undertaken life-union which is lasting, complete and exclusive'.[59] It would go beyond the scope of this chapter to discuss the various elements in this definition. In the specific context of the Seventh Commandment, it is the concluding part of Barth's definition which is especially relevant. For my own part, the only term I would want to emphasise is the central one – 'life-union'.

To describe marriage as a 'life-union' reminds us of two dimensions in particular: one which could be thought of as more 'spatial' or 'horizontal' and the other as more 'temporal' or 'vertical'. In the first place, marriage as a life-union is a complete co-humanity at all levels, a *polyphony' of life*. As the life-union of man and woman in marriage, this life-union has its special inalienable keynote: as a covenant of man and woman it is the communion of love, cohumanly, erotically, sexually. Barth's definition rightly stresses the free mutual choice of love as the *conditio sine qua non* of marriage. While the erotic, sexual dimension of marriage must never be glossed over or underestimated, neither should the marriage covenant ever be reduced to this one level. Marriage is more than a contract to exchange sexual services – a sort of 'limited liability company' restricted exclusively to this level. It is the joining of two lives for real co-existence in all aspects and relationships of life. In the ordinary way, therefore, marriage includes the wider family within the newly drawn circle, establishing a relationship with the generations before and after. But in every case its aim is a complete partnership in which each partner's activities, needs and interests are shared intensively and extensively, and common tasks and interests developed.

But marriage is also a 'life-union' in the temporal sense as a permanent fellowship established for life, 'for keeps'. A 'trial marriage' is really a contradiction in terms, if it means a union in which divorce is regarded as a possibility which is always available. Any built-in licence for divorce is ruled out by the covenant analogy itself. *Exitus non patet*. There is no exit. This will be the motto written above any ethically valid decision to marry, representing at least a sincere intention. The possibility that this intention will not always be realized, that a life-union can become a dead and even murderous business cannot arrogantly be ruled out in any marriage. When this happens, even a divorce can be the better solution, even ethically, for all concerned. To adopt a legalistic attitude here, to cry defiantly

Fiat matrimonium, pereat mundus!, as the church has done for centuries, is hardly any more fruitful here than in other areas. There is no automatic justification for such an attitude on the analogy of the covenant (which was established as a covenant of grace and not as an instrument of bondage). Nevertheless, a rupture of this kind, an abandonment of the marriage covenant, is never to be considered something 'normal', a kind of *intermezzo* which in one way or another forms part of our normal human programme, but only as a failure, a shipwreck, a surrender, which should be forgiven but never justified. For on the basis of creation, and with the central purpose and promise of creation in view, marriage is also a 'life-union' in the sense of a 'life-long' union of man and woman.

It is because marriage is a life-union in this sense of an inclusive and permanent life-covenant, that it is the principal form of the man-woman relationship. It is always within this covenant that *sexuality,* that specific, specially fruitful yet at the same time specially threatened dimension of our common humanity as men and women, is best fulfilled. It receives help and reinforcement from both aspects of a real life-union. It is supported by the total inclusive marriage context, for sexuality only becomes truly human when it is not abstracted and divorced from its context in life as a 'naked fact' but made part of a personal fellowship of a life shared in all its dimensions. 'Coitus without co-existence is demonic.' [60] And it is supported by the striving for permanence in marriage, for sexuality only becomes truly human when it is expressed not at random, out of context, in occasional extra-marital escapades, but in the covenanted bond of personal love, a love which does not flame up spasmodically out of the blue but rather lives, plans, prepares its duration, its history, indeed its eternity. 'All delight demands eternity' – Nietzsche's well-known aphorism captures something of this dimension and thrust of love in the Christian view of marriage.

Freedom from the Tyrannies of Lovelessness

'But life's not like that!' – this protest was long overdue. Surely the Christian view of marriage is hopelessly idealistic and utopian?! When we think of the conditions and the actual

practice of the man-woman relationship today, when we consider the enormous pressures and temptations to which men
and women are exposed today (not just in the matter of
sexuality, of course, but there especially), surely this is too high
an ideal, worse still, one which plainly demands more than the
majority of men and women can give. Certainly if our ethic is
not to be a rather ridiculous haranguing of a non-existent
audience, if it is really to influence real people and provide real
help in the ordering of their lives, these objections must be
taken very seriously indeed. To heed these contemporary
realities is particularly essential when it comes to dealing with
specific fellow human beings who are swept off their feet,
momentarily or permanently, by and who leap more or less
spontaneously on to the modern band-wagon of sex and life,
dedicated to the pursuit of pleasure, acquisition and success.
Much patience and understanding is called for here in Christian
ethics. 'The role of the Church is not that of a moral governess
nor is its purpose to establish a 'tyranny of decency" in
opposition to a "tyranny of indecency".' [61] We are not to use
the commandment 'You shall not commit adultery' as if it were
the cold blade of a moral guillotine.

Yet precisely in the conditions to which we have just alluded,
it is all the more essential to continue to maintain frankly and
unswervingly the validity of the Seventh Commandment. For
this commandment is not a moral guillotine but a signpost to
life, one which is still intended to help human beings as it
always was. It points the way to freedom or, more specifically,
the way to love. This freedom, this love, is threatened by both
the 'tyrannies' just mentioned, which could also be called
tyrannies of lovelessness. The image of 'tyrannies' is suggested
by H. J. Kraus, but the above quotation from him was not
complete. He goes on to present the positive goal to be sought:
Church ethics is challenged 'to convince modern thought of the
dignity and freedom of married fellowship as something
trustworthy, desirable, precious and creative'.[62]

That in fact is our continuing responsibility in this field. It is
rather sad to see theologians losing their nerve at this point and
accommodating themselves to currents of thought which brand
marriage – not just certain outdated forms and aspects of
marriage but marriage as a committed lifelong union of man

and woman – as a burden and an imposition, and by doing so, largely cancelling the validity of the Seventh Commandment. The result is not an increase in freedom, rather the reverse. Certainly it increases the confusion. We have no right to turn the justifiable challenge of those who say 'But life's not like that' into an unwarranted surrender to the pressures of our time. To do so is to forfeit our freedom.

The command 'You shall not commit adultery' points in a different direction. The biblical message is not unmindful of our common human frailty, our vulnerability to temptation; it knows the depths of the human heart. Our sensitivity in this direction is sharpened by what Jesus says about adultery in the Sermon on the Mount. We must also remember here the analogy of the covenant. How often and how 'inventively' God's covenant was broken in the life of God's people. From the biblical standpoint, certainly, this area of tension of our cohumanity as men and women is no playground for the knowalls and the self-righteous. But that makes it all the more helpful to remember that the *covenant holds good:* the covenant of God's fidelity and, in its light, the covenant of our common humanity, and, ultimately and concretely, the covenant of our marriage. This can be assailed from without and within. There can be hours and even years when the positive meaning of it all may become uncertain and obscure to us, when other possibilities beckon seductively to us. The pathway of marriage is not automatically broad and straight but, in fact, often narrow and obscure. We live our marriages 'in the jungle' – of our hearts and our circumstances.

But just here, the clear directive of this commandment can help us. Adultery is a breach of life; it is a possibility, an idea, we are not even to toy with. The commandment protects us from irresponsible impatience with our own marriage, from throwing in our hand too soon by lovelessly abandoning our marriage partner. Certainly this appeal to the liberating history of God's covenant provides no automatic solution to our marriage problem. What it does provide, however, is a perspective which can protect us against momentary pressures and overhasty reactions which however understandable must nevertheless be resisted and overcome. The reference to the divine covenant challenges and encourages us for the long haul

of the love which 'is patient and kind . . . not jealous or
boastful, not arrogant or rude', the love which 'does not insist
on its own way', which is 'not irritable or resentful, does not
rejoice at wrong but rejoices in the right', the love which 'never
ends' (1 Cor.13:4ff.).

The love to which the apostle bears witness here is not to be
equated, of course, with any married love between man and
woman. Yet neither is it to be separated from such married
love. At any rate we are permitted to live our marriage and to
renew and rebuild it again and again within the enfolding reach
and power of this love. This is the vital dimension and purpose
of the Seventh Commandment. In no sense a moral guillotine
but rather an invitation to us never to lose sight of the positive
goal of a permanent life-union in freedom and love – in spite of
everything.

I conclude and summarise with a quotation which seems to
me especially helpful. Surprisingly enough it was written by
one who was himself unmarried (as is often also the case in the
Bible itself when addressing this theme). It may for that very
reason be a timely reminder that the basic concern for the
co-humanity of man and woman is not a monopoly of 'experienced' (or even 'case-hardened'!) married people but the concern of us all.

Writing on the divine commandment in his *Ethics*, Dietrich
Bonhoeffer has this to say about the Seventh Commandment:
'If I love my wife, if I accept my marriage as an institution of
God, then there comes an inner freedom and certainty of life
and action in marriage; I can no longer watch with suspicion
every step that I take; I no longer call in question every deed
that I perform. The divine prohibition of adultery is then no
longer the centre round which all my thought and action in
marriage revolves. (As though the meaning and purpose of
marriage consisted in nothing except the avoidance of
adultery!) But it is the free honouring and the free acceptance
of marriage, the leaving behind of the prohibition of adultery,
which is now the precondition of the fulfilment of the divine
commission of marriage. The divine commandment has here
become the permission to live in marriage in freedom and
certainty'.[63]

THE EIGHTH COMMANDMENT:
You Shall Not Steal

Focus on Kidnapping

'It is high time that the reliable findings of biblical scholarship prevailed over the established traditional interpretation in our understanding of Ex.20:15. Once Albrecht Alt's essay on "The Prohibition of Theft in the Decalogue" was published in 1953, theological ethics no longer had any justification for failing to take account of the new interpretation which arises out of the context of the Torah. More astonishing than even this failure is the distrust – symptomatic of Christian theology – of Jewish biblical scholarship, whose findings even Alt did not have before him. What the Talmud says is this: "Our masters taught: You shall not steal! The Scripture is speaking here of the theft of human beings" (Sanhedrin 86s).' [64]

Hans Joachim Kraus's forthright comment marks a really spectacular breakthrough in the history of the interpretation of the Decalogue. Ecclesiastical exegesis of the Eighth Commandment in sermons, catechisms, and even text books on ethics has almost without exception taken the words 'You shall not steal' to refer in a quite general way to all offences against property as prohibiting all unlawful expropriation of another person's property. But such an interpretation is challenged or at least modified by recent Old Testament scholarship and by the ancient Jewish tradition, whose approach to the commandment is much more concrete. What is prohibited here is not theft in general but one particular form of theft, namely, kidnapping, i.e. the theft or enslavement of an Israelite human being.

There are substantial arguments in support of this view. In the first place there are *exegetical* grounds: the most immediate comment on the Eighth Commandment is undoubtedly to be found in Ex.21:16 which reads: 'Whoever steals a man, whether he sells him or is found in possession of him, shall be put to death'. We should also compare Deut.24:7. Some memory of the infamous sale of Joseph by his brothers may be part of the background here, but also and above all, of course, the Exodus context of the Decalogue itself. The 'Ten Great Freedoms' accompany the nation of former slaves which had had to endure all the bitterness of oppression in the Egyptian house of bondage. It is impossible for the 'signpost to freedom' to ignore this experience nor has it any desire to ignore it. It addresses itself therefore to this sombre reality of kidnapping and slavery, directly and centrally. There can be no surrender of the newly bestowed freedom, at this vital point least of all. It is not difficult, therefore, to understand the specific focus of this Eighth Commandment: No kidnapping, no slavery, ever again, among the people of God!

There are *structural* grounds, too, to support this interpretation. To understand the Eighth Commandment as referring to kidnapping also settles the problem of the 'overlapping' which many modern exegetes find between the Eighth and the Tenth Commandments. 'You shall not covet your neighbour's house . . .' The Tenth Commandment obviously has in view the temptations connected with property. A further point is that, on the kidnapping hypothesis, the Second Table of the Decalogue gains in inner coherence and clarity. 'The inner connection of the last five commands of the Decalogue clearly emerges only when we see that each of them secures a basic right of the free citizen of Israel. Starting with the Sixth Commandment, these are: life, marriage, freedom, honour and property.' [65]

From the traditional standpoint of Christian ethics, this exegetical focus on kidnapping may at first sight seem rather off-putting, And, indeed, until quite recent times, there would have been some grounds for complaining that this 'new' interpretation entails a lamentable loss of relevance and realism. Offences against property are a constant preoccupation, it could be argued, but which of us is concerned with such barbaric ancient customs as kidnapping? But does the Eighth Commandment, understood in this 'new' way, really leave us unscathed today? Yet today it is the latter question which

strikes us as being rhetorical. Because of certain spectacular
recent cases we are all of us unhappily aware that, in the matter
of kidnapping in particular, we are far closer to those 'barbaric
times' than we had allowed ourselves to believe.

I am referring, of course, to the *problem of the terrorists.*
Kidnapping in the sense of taking hostages for purposes of
blackmail was not something invented in the recent wave of
terrorism. This form of blackmail appears over and over again
in the history of civilization: the taking of hostages and their
execution in wartime, for example, or the various forms of
'kidnapping' used by gangsters as a 'conventional' means of
securing the payment of very high ransoms. The terrorist scene
is really nothing new under the western sun. The relatively new
thing which has been happening under our very eyes – literally
so, since television coverage brings these events vividly and
often excessively right into our living rooms – is the elevation
of kidnapping to the status of general 'political' strategy. Nor
can this strategy be denied its success, a truly ominous and
dubious success. Powerful governments have been paralyzed
for weeks, even months; government institutions have been
shaken and countless citizens made insecure. Understandably,
governments at the same time organize defensive counter-
measures and in their wake reactionary 'counter-trends' take
on a new lease of life, with the result that the prospects of a
creative human development of social opportunities recede
rather than come nearer. Experience shows that the game of
political kidnapping is a sickness which leads to political death.
Political murder leads – at first in the extended sense – to
political suicide.

Against such a background, the Eighth Commandment in its
original sense becomes remarkably relevant in the contemporary world. 'You shall not steal a human being!' The theft of a
fellow human being is categorically excluded as an ethical and
political option, and with special severity (we have only to
recall the commentary of Ex.21:16 and Deut.24:7, where, in
contrast to offences against property, kidnapping is punishable
by death). We are not at liberty to use a human life as a means
to an end, to put pressure on or extort money from others. The
use of such a means corrupts the most laudable cause. The
evasion of this principle always has disastrous consequences.

The Eighth Commandment cuts cleanly through all sophistry here and makes the situation quite clear. It is all the more to be regretted, therefore, that its radical incisiveness has been blunted in the history of interpretation, i.e. by stressing its general application to offences against property. The theologians and interpreters thereby deprived contemporary morality and politics of an important ethical and political emphasis and it is high time, therefore, to make good this deficiency.

Pressures in the Direction of Slavery

The backlog to be made good is to be understood comprehensively, of course. It is not simply a question of the taking of hostages by terrorists. Certainly terrorism is a particularly dramatic and obnoxious form of kidnapping, but it is only the tip of the iceberg. The protection afforded by the Eighth Commandment extends much further than the enclaves of national and international terrorism. It also takes in all those open and even disguised ways in which human beings are robbed of their freedom. Recalling the Exodus and the deliverance it brought to Israel, we have to think here concretely and historically of *slavery*. Caution is called for here, of course, since the Old Testament contains no explicit or general prohibition of slavery. On the contrary, the institution of slavery was accepted in Israel as it was in the Orient and in antiquity generally, particularly in the case of foreign slaves. The Exodus event nevertheless remained an eloquent summons to the covenant people to continue to be a nation of free people. There are constant exhortations to keep this in mind: 'You shall remember that you were a slave in Egypt' (Deut.15:15). 'This memory explains why the legislation concerning slavery in Israel is clearly biassed in favour of the slaves . . . All the legal provisions dealing with slaves are designed either to improve their lot or to reduce the duration of their servitude. On the other hand, there is not a single law protecting the property rights of the slave-owner.' [66] The way of freedom is undoubtedly the divinely appointed way for humanity; first of all for the covenant people, but then, too, for *all* human beings – in the eschatological promise the other peoples are not excluded. At this point the New Testament picks up the story. In Christ we are set free and called to freedom (Gal.5:1) and in him 'there is neither Jew nor Greek, there is neither slave nor free, there is neither male nor female' (Gal.3:28).

We cannot ignore the fact, of course, that this promise and gift of freedom in Christ did not automatically lead to the abolition of slavery. Given the eschatologically foreshortened perspective of the primitive Church and the pressure of existing social and economic conditions, a call for the abolition of the institution of slavery was scarcely conceivable, much less attainable. Yet, as Paul's letter to Philemon shows in one specific case, the system of slavery was undermined from within by the practice of genuine solidarity across the class barriers. The primitive Christian communities, 'Oases of a life without oppression' (as Gollwitzer calls them), were pioneers in producing models of community life pointing the way to greater human fellowship and solidarity, and so to greater freedom and justice. Here, on the basis of the Gospel, an explosive charge was inserted into the very foundations of slavery and other institutionalized forms of kidnapping.

The historical scandal of Christendom is that this 'explosive charge' was never allowed to operate fully in the subsequent course of 'Christian civilization' but was over and over again sandbagged and restricted and defused, and that to some extent this was done with the ideological support of official theology. One eloquent and deplorable illustration of this is that it should have been possible for 'Christian nations' to engage in the slave trade right down into the last century and, with the aid of modern technology, even to develop new forms of slavery, as for example in the enslavement of the African peoples and their transportation in unspeakable conditions across the seas to America. The real meaning of 'kidnapping' was uncovered here in a particularly monstrous and cruel way. Did the blunting of the sharp cutting edge of the Eighth Commandment perhaps contribute here, too, to the havoc wrought in this context?

The historical institution of slavery has almost completely disappeared from our world today. But it would be foolish to suppose this to mean that the problems addressed by the Eighth Commandment no longer concern us. The alarming reality of 'stealing human beings' has certainly not been eliminated simply because the institution of slavery has been effectively challenged and largely abolished in practice. 'Kidnapping' can take many different forms. We need only listen to the voices of the 'former slaves' – both historically and geographically close to the victims of slavery – of those Third World nations discriminated against and colonially exploited because of their race. It is not *their* view that the abolition of the slave trade or even the ending of overt colonialism means that kidnapping and the theft of their freedom is over for them. More subtle forms of neo-colonialisation have replaced the old, and even the old forms still have their impregnable strongholds. Consider the system of apartheid. The ecumenical 'programme to combat racism' takes on an abiding significance in this context. Despite all its controversial aspects, it can provide, for all who are willing to learn, a very powerful and long overdue stimulus to an ethical reorientation in the direction of the original thrust of the Eighth Commandment.

There are features not only of the 'Third World' but also of the other two 'worlds' today which come within the scope of the Eighth Commandment and its application. A very impressive report on the 'Second World' can be found, for example, in Solzhenitsyn's *Gulag Archipelago*. His book is in fact an extended commentary on the depressing validity of the Eighth Commandment in the Stalinist and neo-Stalinist era. But we should not confine our attention to other countries. Other forms of kipnapping are constantly appearing in our own societies, not to speak of terrorism. In the Swiss Law, for example, crimes involving the 'theft of freedom' are defined as 'the wilful and unlawful withdrawal of a person's freedom of movement by imprisonment or some other means' (violence, hypnotism, etc.). Here again we need to remember that what can be brought within the scope of the criminal code represents only the tip of the iceberg. Is not our 'ordinary' working world and consumer society permeated with more subtle pressures which nonetheless involve the 'theft of human beings', their deprivation of freedom? This, too, is something to be examined by theologians seeking to interpret the Eighth Commandment, and here again there is much leeway to be made up. Marxist thinking, despite all its partiality and the narrow ideological nostrums to which it has sometimes stooped, has analyzed and attacked the mechanisms of economic and social 'kidnapping' far more thoroughly and vigorously than the Christian social moralists have done. We must present these challenges in our preaching of the Eighth Commandment today. They constitute part of its direct reference to our actual world. 'What happens in the factories and on the assembly lines is placed in the light of God's commandment.' [67] We shall be wise, indeed we are commanded, not to blunt the original incisive thrust and cutting edge of the command 'You shall not steal' and its direct application to 'kidnapping'.

Theft 'from above' and theft 'from below'

In our interpretation of the Eighth Commandment so far, we have followed the direction indicated by recent Old Testament scholarship and interpreted the commandment as a prohibition of kidnapping. In comparison with the conventional interpretation, this enhanced rather than reduced the relevance of the commandment. But the question now arises as to what we are to make of the traditional interpretation, the general prohibition of theft. Was the Church quite mistaken in its traditional teaching? Do offences against property lie outside the scope of Ex.20:15 or even of the Decalogue as a whole? Is the logical step to abandon the theological criticism of theft or else to deal with it under the tenth and last commandment?

There are tendencies in church and society today to give an affirmative response to these questions, and this not only on exegetical grounds but also and above all on general cultural, historical and ethical grounds. In comparison with the sombre aspects of kidnapping, the everyday realities envisaged in the conventional prohibition of theft seem to many of our contemporaries to be mere trivialities, mere peccadilloes, of quite minor importance. They find it difficult to accept the obligation to take the commandment seriously in everyday life. Again and again we find ourselves in a grey area where extremely dubious and often rather hazy economic and financial intrigues are commonplace, from dishonest tax declarations to major banking scandals, from the misuse of other people's property to cases of illegitimate profit and corruption. Nor does all this strike us as happening in an alien world of criminality outside us but rather as almost an element of our modern 'life-style'. We have only to consider, for example, the high incidence of shoplifting in affluent societies but also the high rate of thefts from theological (!) college libraries, unpaid-for bus rides and the pilfering that goes on in offices and factories (even by socialist workers acting on the unofficial slogan of many who work in nationalized industries that 'Anyone who doesn't steal is letting his family down!'). Trivialities? Peccadilloes? Of minor importance? In such 'jungle' conditions people find it fairly easy to rid themselves of a bad conscience. Surely even theological accusations are out of place here?

The theologian's first duty here, it seems to me, is to make distinctions and to insist on clear thinking. To select and condemn isolated instances often turns out in fact to be an indulgence in fallacious ethical over-simplification. We weaken the seriousness and credibility of our interpretation of the commandment when we leave the context out of account or operate on the principle that 'petty thieves are hung, ambitious ones are knighted!' We cannot ignore the concrete conditions and contexts of theft. At this point, moreover, the traditional interpretation of the Eighth Commandment has often been extremely realistic and down to earth. Consider, for example, the lively passage in Luther's *Large Catechism:* 'This (i.e. theft) is the commonest craft and the largest guild on earth and if we regard the world throughout all conditions of life, it is nothing else than a vast, wide stall full of great thieves . . . Yet, here we might be silent about the trifling individual thieves if we were to attack the great, powerful arch-thieves with whom lords and princes keep company, who daily plunder not only a city or two, but all Germany'.[68]

It is encouraging and welcome that one of the most influential catechisms of the Reformation, and even earlier, the reformist preaching of a Jan Hus and a whole current of the 'first Reformation', i.e. that of the Waldensians and the Hussites, should have grasped the true scope of the Eighth Commandment in this sense. It counteracted the very strong temptation to settle for a narrow moralistic interpretation (e.g. for moralistic condemnations of the 'petty thief' while showing indulgence for the 'large scale thief'). This tradition was also

one on which the religious socialists were able to build their
own interpretation with its recurring reference to 'thievish
elements' in the structures of society. To give just one example,
from the catechism of L. Ragaz: 'Financial intrigue to the
disadvantage of the masses is theft. Capital regarded as an end
and a goal for a profit economy is theft. The exploitation of
housing, clothing, food and drink, gambling and entertainment,
of human beings by speculation for profit, is theft. The confis-
cation of land belonging to people by another people, i.e. every
form of imperialism and, in particular, the former colonial
system, is theft'.[69]

If a contemporary ethic is to be realistic it must develop and
command this comprehensive sense of the commandment,
'You shall not steal'. In doing so it will also tackle the question
of the social system and social conditions – not by blanket
condemnations based on ideological prejudices but by continually pressing for the unmasking and elimination of the 'thievish
elements', by a discriminating opposition to the onesided
profit-oriented 'capitalistic' element in our system. The Eighth
Commandment must certainly never be interpreted solely in
terms of social ethics, too. An ethic which takes its cue from the
Decalogue will necessarily become social ethics.

But we must avoid false alternatives here. The Eighth Commandment has its inherent concretely personal, indeed individual focus. We are not to play the structural aspect off against
the personal, or *vice versa*. We cannot appeal to the prevailing
morality to excuse or even justify our own personal breaches of
the commandment; for example, by adopting the familiar
dictum: 'Comrades, socialism will be hard; let's make the best
of capitalism!' There must be no unilateral neutralization of the
personal applications of the Eighth Commandment. 'With this
commandment', says Walter Lüthi, 'God meddles in our financial affairs'. When it comes to the 'minor infringements'
referred to earlier, it won't do to talk of 'trivialities',
'peccadilloes' or 'petty offences'. A doctored tax declaration is
not a petty offence but fraud. A stolen theological book not a
trivial matter but theft. Riding the bus without paying your fare
is not a mere bagatelle or a sport but (as the notices in Basle
trams say) 'unfair'. To resist all this and a whole lot more in the
jungle of daily life is not just 'puritanism' but matches the

thrust and scope of the Eighth Commandment. Even our most private acts dealing with property – our own, that of our fellow human beings, that of society – fall within the scope of the imperative 'You shall not steal'. There are no private enclaves where its validity is automatically suspended.

If we recall what was said in the first part of this chapter on the subject of kidnapping, we can focus more clearly this whole vast area of offences against property and get the ethical emphasis right. The Eighth Commandment begins, as I said, with the concrete cases of kidnapping, but then, its directive continues, with logical consistency, to extend to the area of institutional slavery and other crude forms of oppression, and then to take in more subtle ways of exploiting people and depriving them of their freedom. It is precisely as this extension is continued that we see the full import of the problems of theft in all their range. In concerning itself with these wider problems in its theology and ethics, the Church was not just dealing with secondary matters. 'The relationship with things and the relationship with human beings do not in fact run along parallel lines which never meet. Above all from the standpoint of freedom, they are inseparable.' [70] The human being is never an abstract self-contained individual but always at the same time 'the human world', 'the ensemble of the social relations' (Karl Marx).[71] There is a connection between human freedom – and the theft of human freedom – and economic and property relationships, and *vice versa,* of course. Only in this anthropological context does the problem of theft acquire its ethical importance. Not because 'property is sacred' – the proper place for a commandment understood in that sense would be in the law code not of the living God of liberation but of a fetishized idol – but because 'human life is sacred'.

The Janus face of property

Here we have to consider *property* as a theological problem. 'In the Eighth Commandment, God protects property. He protects it against theft of every kind . . . But, does God protect property of every kind? Even property acquired unjustly? In the Eighth Commandment, is God only protecting the haves from the have-nots, against theft "from below", so to speak? This is what has always been assumed in the traditional interpretation of the commandment. But is it not the case, rather, that in this commandment God is also protecting the have-nots against the greed of the haves, so to speak against "theft from above"?' [72]

In the light of the biblical testimony, the only answer to Lüthi's question is: 'Yes, God is also protecting the have-nots from the haves'. But the biblical signpost keeps both these forms of theft in view, even if the main stress in its prophetic warning is on the prohibition of theft 'from above'. There is a close connection between this and the dialectic of the biblical view of property. It is true that the Bible does not particularly stress that property has a positive significance but almost takes it for granted that it forms part – or could form part – of the most basic requirements of earthly life. Humanity in the Old Testament delights in possessions, considers them a mark of divine blessing and thanks God for the possibilities they open up. In the New Testament, too, both in the gospels and the epistles, it is assumed that people possess property, dispose of it, work with it, even increase it (e.g. Lk.19:11f.; Mt.20:15). There is no biblical basis for considering property as demonic, equating it directly with humanity's lapses into sin, as they sometimes have been in certain strands of socialist and communist tradition in Europe, for quite understandable reasons. 'Having' is obviously integral to human 'being' in history, part indeed of its built-in biological defence against need. Unlike our fellow creatures, who are 'equipped' by nature for their mode of life, we human beings can only survive by fabricating our basic necessities of life from our environment and possessing the elementary equipment for life. In this sense, personal property is an indispensable condition for the development of human life.

But there is a huge difference between affirming the need for property on the basis of anthropology and glorifying it unconditionally or even canonizing it (as has happened over long stretches of recent history on the basis of the bourgeois tradition). The biblical view of property and its problems reveals a Janus-faced reality. Its *negative* aspects are not to be ignored. We are not to forget the prophetic 'counterpoint'. It is to this set of problems that some of the most serious warnings of the biblical witnesses are repeatedly directed – in Amos,

Deuteronomy, as well as in the teaching of Jesus and the apostles. Both objectively and subjectively, we human beings, we Christians, are without doubt especially frail and vulnerable, especially endangered, especially easily dehumanised, precisely here in our handling of property and our attitude to possessions.

Objectively: property is misused whenever it turns into an instrument of power over our fellow human beings instead of being an aid to ensure human life and development. It is especially easy for this to happen in this field, and for it to be practised with consummate greed. The person who is strong economically, the person who owns the means of production, acquires power over labour, over social production – and therefore over human beings. Justice and peace, and with them human solidarity, are threatened by the need and distress of the oppressed, the underprivileged, those who have become dependent. This is the point of the prophetic protest and of Jesus' identification with the poor and the oppressed. At the same time, however, especially in the New Testament, attention is directed to the *subjective* aspects of the misuse of property. The power of property can destroy the humanity not only of the poor but also of the rich. This happens, above all, when the 'law of accumulation' which is so strong in the realm of property becomes for the rich the law of their life. When 'possessing' and the desire to possess become not just a means to life, to 'being', but are transformed into the real goal of life, humanity is assailed and crippled, that of the possessor, the rich human being, especially. Confronted with this 'capitalist delusion', Jesus speaks of the power of Mammon and leaves us in no doubt that we are confronted here with a straight choice: one or the other, but not both. We recall the saying of Jesus, already quoted in our exposition of the First Commandment: 'No one can serve two masters . . . You cannot serve God and Mammon' (Mt.6:24). Certainly we are not to equate property with the 'root evil', yet this 'root evil' certainly has particularly fatal consequences in the field of property. Theologically, therefore, the problem of property is certainly a Janus-faced problem.

It is with this field of tension that the Eighth Commandment is concerned. It offers no easy ready-made solutions for the problems of our economic, legal, financial and private life. But what it does do is to open up the fundamental standpoint, the 'signpost to freedom', in a compelling and liberating way. Freedom is its concern, its *cantus firmus* and at the same time the clamp which holds the *two* dimensions of its interpretation together in an organic whole. The Eighth Commandment protects our *right* to life and freedom against attacks from our fellow human beings. Whether the threat is an elementary and brutal threat, such as kidnapping, or a more devious and subtle threat, that of economic oppression, the commandment sharpens our awareness of the threat. It is because of this basic concern for freedom and in order to secure this freedom that we are commanded: 'You shall not steal.' In this command as in the entire Decalogue, it is the defence and the practice of freedom which is at stake.

The comprehensive scope of the commandment calls for an equally comprehensive strategy in obeying it. This strategy will include an alert individual conscience which refuses to swim with the stream of 'petty crime'. But it will also include a social and political commitment which seeks 'to overthrow all those conditions in which humanity is a debased, enslaved, neglected and contemptible being' (to quote Karl Marx, who really has some authority in this field!).[73] Both elements are part of freedom's response to the divine philanthropic directive: 'You shall not steal'.

One concluding remark. It is striking that there should be no direct reference to the Eighth Commandment in the Sermon on the Mount, which is a radical interpretation of some of the commandments of the Decalogue. The Sermon contains a clear reference to the Sixth Commandment: 'You have heard that it was said to the men of old: You shall not kill . . .' (Mt.5:21ff.). Then the Seventh Commandment is dealt with: 'You shall not commit adultery . . .' (Mt.5:27). There is even a reference to the Ninth: 'You shall not swear falsely . . .' (Mt.5:33). But the Eighth Commandment is conspicuous by its absence. Should this absence be regretted?

Perhaps. But Jesus has not left us completely without guidance here. Quite apart from the whole context of the Gospel in which, as we pointed out, the temptation to avarice and to the exploitation of our fellow human beings is repeatedly denounced, Jesus does in fact speak incisively and authoritatively on this theme, even if he makes no direct reference to the Eighth Commandment. To learn Jesus' basic attitude in this field, we have only to read the Beatitudes (Mt.5:1-12) in this light. The poor, the meek (of whom it is said that they will 'inherit the earth'), those who hunger for bread and justice, the merciful – these are the ones who are set here in the floodlight of the Gospel promise. They reflect conditions of life and ways of behaving which are at the same time in stark contrast to the practice of 'robbery' and 'theft'. And in the later parts of the Gospel we cannot miss the tremendous warning against Mammonism of every kind, in which indeed all that requires to be said about the Eighth Commandment is epitomized: 'Do not lay up for yourselves treasures on earth, where moth and rust consume and where thieves break through and steal, but lay up for yourselves treasures in heaven, where neither moth nor rust consumes and where thieves do not break through and steal. For where your treasure is, there will your heart be also . . . You cannot serve God and Mammon' (Mt.6:19ff.).

THE NINTH COMMANDMENT:

Truth for the Neighbour

Witnessing to the Truth

When we come to the next-to-last commandment of the
Decalogue, we are perhaps tempted to exclaim: 'What an
anti-climax!' 'When they reach this point, in fact, many expositions of the Ten Commandments seem to suggest that the bulk
of the harvest is now already safely gathered in and that from
the Ninth Commandment onwards, it is only a matter of a not
very rewarding gleaning process, a mere epilogue.' [74] The
plausibility of this view seems to be enhanced when a comparison is made with the preceding commandments. These dealt
with important aspects of life – life itself, marriage, property, –
in other words, with obvious, 'tangible' human concerns,
whereas the Ninth Commandment is concerned merely with
'verbal' offences.

Such a conclusion must be firmly resisted. The Ninth Commandment is not concerned merely with 'verbal' offences but
with the truth of human life. As such, it is no mere secondary
coda or appendix to the preceding commandments but a
central commandment in its own right. Perhaps this is just
prejudice on my part. My thinking here rests on a very definite
assumption, one which was particularly characteristic of the
Czech Reformation. The theme of truth, or more specifically,
the witness to truth, played a vital part in that Reformation.
We therefore find this theme constantly recurring with striking
force at crucial points in the history of the Czech churches and
the Czech civilization.

As background illustrations, I want now to refer to *three
names,* providing evidence of the relevance of the Ninth Commandment to real life and its obligations. First and foremost,
Jan Hus. For this Czech Reformer, the truth *(pravda)* is the key

theme of doctrine and life. In chapter 5 of his *'Interpretation of Faith'*, he sets out his programme very clearly: 'Faithful Christians, seek the truth, listen to the truth, speak the truth, cleave to the truth, defend the truth to the death!' This was not just airy rhetoric. As Hus saw it, concern for the truth, described here in all its facets, is the really fundamental dimension of Christian life. To live by evading the truth is not a trivial matter; it means the loss of the centre, the meaning, the goal of human life, and this is worse than the loss of physical life itself. For the truth is not a merely 'verbal' matter but, because Christ is the truth, the fundamental condition of our salvation. This explains why Hus did not shrink back from carrying his belief to its logical conclusion, however badly things might turn out for him. Accused before the Council of Constance, he refused to recant the truth he saw, and so he became a martyr, a blood witness to the truth.

My second example is *Thomas G. Masaryk,* the humanist philosopher, politician and founder of the Czech State, and, in addition to all this, a man of impressive personal integrity in all the spheres of life just mentioned. Masaryk's integrity, directly linked in part with Jan Hus, was anchored in his attitude to truth, which laid special emphasis on consistency and sincerity right down into the details of everyday life and conduct. The writer Karel Capek found this keynote of Masaryk's life illustrated in the following anecdote. During the Russian Revolution, Masaryk found himself in the open street in Moscow, caught between the crossfire of both sides. Under the hail of bullets, he managed to reach the entrance to a hotel and asked to be admitted. But the porter kept the door closed: 'Are you one of our guests? If you're not, you can't enter. We're full up!' 'I didn't want to tell a lie', Masaryk related, 'so I shouted to the porter: 'Don't be foolish, open the door!' The porter admitted him. What left a permanent impression on Capek in this anecdote, was the offhand parenthesis, 'I didn't want to tell a lie' – even when his life was in danger.

The third example is that of *Jan Palach,* the young Czech student, unknown until the day of his death, who immolated himself in Wenceslas Square in Prague in January 1969 as a protest against the depressing turn in Czech political life following the Soviet intervention. Palach's gesture shocked the entire Czech nation, as well as many people in neighbouring and distant lands. People were puzzled as to the immediate motives for this self-sacrifice. But Palach's friends were in no doubt about the deeper dimension, for one of Palach's last conversations with his pastor was about Christ's words: 'For this I was born . . . to bear witness to the truth' (Jn.18:37). It was clearly along these lines that Jan Palach wished to understand his life and his final testimony: 'to bear witness to the truth' is the vital concern of the Christian life, more important than all other concerns, personal or political.

These are three very different examples of three very different people. Yet all three have one thing in common: the truth is the vital element and atmosphere of human life. In the question of truth, what is at stake is not just the 'predicates' of our human existence but its 'subject', our true identity as human beings in the presence of God and of our fellow human beings. When this is recognized, it also becomes clear that the Ninth Commandment is no marginal signpost to freedom but a central and indispensable one. In what direction does it point us?

Life as a Judicial Process

'You shall not bear false witness against your neighbour.' In trying to understand this commandment, we find ourselves in a situation similar to that which confronted us in dealing with the Eighth Commandment. In the main, the traditional interpretation goes beyond the original meaning of the text of the Decalogue. This may not necessarily be wrong, but it will be advisable to examine and reflect first of all on the original more restricted meaning. What is the original reference? 'For all who are familiar with the original text, the Ninth Commandment clearly has in view witness in court proceedings, and not lying in general. This needs always to be borne in mind as a counter to overhasty interpretations of the commandment in the direction of lying in general . . . The extension of the scope of the commandment to include this wider area can only be a second step. Yet this step can be taken with a good conscience not simply because false witness is itself an extreme instance of lying but also because the Old Testament, by frequently defining false witness as 'lying witness', clearly considers the essence of false witness to be the lie at the heart of it.' [75]

The situation primarily envisaged in the Ninth Commandment is that in *a court of law,* i.e. the emergency situation of the search for the truth, when someone's testimony will determine whether a fellow human being is acquitted or condemned, and sometimes whether he will live or die. It was this situation which was 'the source or origin from which the blessing of truth and the corruption of falsehood spread out into the life of the people'.[76] The Bible offers an impressive picture of just how evil the effects of false witness can be. It does so, moreover, not just at its margins but in the very centre of its New Testament message. I am thinking here of the trial of Jesus and of the role played in it by the false witnesses (Mk.14:55f.). Sad to say, this primary application of the Ninth Commandment is more relevant than ever today. One of the most depressing of contemporary experiences is the spectacle of manipulated pseudo show trials so frequently staged by totalitarian régimes of every hue, despite diminishing returns in the way of credibility. On this stage, false witnesses appear with monotonous regularity.

Such things are a direct affront to Christian ethics; not just to personal ethical standards by which the Christian is forbidden ever to take the way of false witness, but also to social ethical standards, too, in the sense that we are called to strive for the establishment of a legal and penal system which places the obligation to discover the truth above all other possible interests and which strives to prevent and eliminate as far as possible all manipulation of justice – all 'false witness against the neighbour'. A lively concern for the legal system, its institutions and the way they function, is part of our common ethical and political responsibility. And this not indirectly but directly, i.e. on the basis of the original meaning of the Ninth Commandment. Justification *and* justice, this is an essential theme of theological ethics, the neglect of which can only be disobedience. The cynical idea that 'good lawyers make bad Christians', while it may be directed against self-opinionated legal practitioners or to the problems which the aspect of justification can present to a committed legal mind, cannot be allowed to stand as a general axiom. Far from running counter to the Christian faith, a humane jurisprudence and a corresponding legal system are in keeping with its supreme interest.

We have every reason to take this concrete approach of the Ninth Commandment, its court-room setting, seriously, and to reckon with it in ethics and politics. But at the same time we have to go further. The concrete approach of the Ninth Commandment is not restricted to the emergency situation in the court-room. It points beyond this to other aspects of our human life. It is not only in confrontation with the law and its representatives in the court-room that we meet the 'trial situation'. This situation exists in many other areas of life, indeed, in our life as a whole. I am not thinking here just of the theological aspect of this situation, i.e. of our life as lived *coram Deo* and ultimately in prospect of the 'Last Judgement' but rather of our ordinary everyday life where we are deeply involved in processes of accusation, prosecution and punishment over wide areas of our life.

This *condition humaine* has been memorably described by some of the great writers of the last generation; above all, of course, by Franz Kafka and Albert Camus. For *Kafka*, 'The Trial' – omnipresent, obscure, oppressive – comes to represent the keynote of our existence, and certainly of life in the alienating conditions of modern society if not of the universal human condition. *Camus* is chiefly concerned with the anticipation of the Last Judgement by human judges: 'God is not needed to create guilt or to punish. Our fellowmen suffice, aided by ourselves. You were speaking of the Last Judgement. Allow me to laugh respectfully. I shall wait for it resolutely for I have known what is worse, the judgement of men'.[77]

It is vital here not to think only of our 'wicked' fellow human beings but to examine closely our own active cooperation in this 'Trial', for all of us are in some measure parties in this case, though our roles are constantly changing. Sometimes we ourselves are exposed to the accusation and condemnation of others; at other times, often without fully realizing it, we ourselves don the mantle of the prosecutor or even of the sentencing judge in the 'Trial' of other people's lives. There are social systems which aim to establish and even succeed in establishing a more or less complete 'appraisal system' reach-

ing down to the most absurd details, in an attempt to understand and analyse its citizens as exhaustively as possible without their knowing this is being done or by whom. I am thinking
of the 'cadre system' in Eastern Europe. But even in the more
open societies of the West, we are aware of similar tendencies.
Thirty years ago, Walter Lüthi was able to point to similar
dangers in Switzerland. In his interpretation of the Ninth
Commandment, he says: 'Think of the enormous role played
by information and enquiry services today. We live in an age of
dossiers and files, of vague phone calls and handwriting
analysis, even of psychiatric reports. Judgements are passed on
people which may dog them for years and years, even their
whole life long . . . Judgements which no human being has the
right to pass on another, but only God himself'.[78]

God's final judgement often seems to be anticipated in fact
by human beings. Nor is this trial, this process, yet complete . . . far from it! It is already developing a new range of
possibilities, very ambiguous in character, as a result of
'technological progress' in our increasingly sophisticated 'data
processing systems'.

Nor is it only in personal human relationships that we
anticipate the 'Last Judgement'. We also do so in institutionalized aspects of our public social life. 'The public platform of
our social life is turned into a tribunal every day . . . Sometimes
it is the journalist who plays the part of public prosecutor, bring
the charges, calling the witnesses, demanding punishment . . .
The "Last Judgement" takes place every day. In earlier times
we used to say: "It is a fearful thing to fall into the hands of the
living God". There are many people today who know how
fearful it is to fall into the hands of other human beings.'[79]

Certainly we are not to make the greater openness displayed
by the mass media in a democratic society the scapegoat here.
This greater 'openness' can be a real power for good. Think of
the liberating role played by the mass media in Czechoslovakia
towards the end of the sixties, or even of the role of the press in
unmasking the Nixon 'lie system' at the time of the Watergate
affair. These positive potentialities are not to be underrated;
the loss of them is often brought home to us in painful ways.
Nor must we lose sight of the other side of the coin, however,
namely, the abuse of the potentialities in the direction of a

manipulated 'Last Judgement'. In this important area of daily life, democratic vigilance is called for also and above all from the standpoint of the Ninth Commandment.

Advocacy in Favour of the Neighbour and of Grace

What guidance can we receive from the Ninth Commandment (and in the light of its New Testament presentation) in the dimensions we have considered? I would like to point out three emphases:

1. In the 'trial situations' of our human life, the Ninth Commandment takes our neighbour's part, is on the side of the person who is our 'trial partner' at any given moment. For if there is one striking feature of this Ninth Commandment which makes it stand out from the Decalogue as a whole, it is that it does not simply repeat the succinct formula of the preceding commandments, does not say, for example, 'You shall not tell lies', but is formulated with explicit reference to the neighbour. 'You shall not bear false witness *against your neighbour*'. We shall have to come back to this point when we reflect on what 'speaking the truth' means. What calls for consideration here is the specific application of the commandment to the field of our apparently incurable litigiousness. Here it sharpens our respect for the dignity and honour of our fellow human beings, assailed from all sides. 'What is at stake in the Ninth Commandment is human dignity, which is far more closely protected by the explicit prohibition of false witness than it would have been by a general proscription of lying.'[80] How easily and swiftly a neighbour's honour and dignity are damaged by false rumours, malicious interpretations of his or her behaviour, the overhasty imputation of motives. All this can happen in a court of law, in an irresponsible sensationalist kind of journalism, but also in our ordinary everyday dealings with one another.

By putting the neighbour's rights and dignity in the forefront, the Ninth Commandment counters these destructive tendencies in our daily life. A provisional summary of the directive of the Ninth Commandment could be that sound principle of classic jurisprudence *in dubio pro reo* (the accused is to be given the benefit of the doubt). This maxim must be adopted not only in the technical administration of justice, though with special stringency there, of course, and the Christian ethic requires us to oppose all infringements in this field. But we must also adopt it very concretely in our personal dealings with our fellow human beings. It is vital here to advance wherever possible beyond mere defence to the positive, a concern which is very evident in Luther's *Large Catechism:* 'For it is a common evil plague that everyone prefers hearing evil to hearing good of his neighbour; and although we ourselves are so bad that we cannot suffer that anyone should say anything bad about us, but everyone would much rather that all the world should speak of him in golden terms, yet we cannot bear that the best is spoken about others'. No one, therefore, should 'publicly judge and reprove his neighbour . . . For there is a great difference between these two things: judging sin and knowing sin. You may indeed know it but you are not to judge it'.[81] In Luther's vivid words, it is firstly a matter of turning our ears into a 'grave' so as to prevent any rumour from snowballing, and secondly 'always to explain advantageously and to put the best construction on all we may hear of a neighbour'.[82] To practise this advocacy of the neighbour amid the ordinary 'trials' of life is the first directive of the Ninth Commandment.

2. The actual practice of this advocacy in favour of the neighbour carries us further in the direction of a fundamental *advocacy of grace* in human society. Our mutual and apparently incurable litigiousness betrays a fatal inclination to mercilessness. We do not merely judge but also condemn. We anticipate the Last Judgement and take it into our own hands. This fatal tendency is plain disobedience to the Ninth Commandment which shatters the supposed logic and consistency of our 'lawsuits'. This contradiction becomes even clearer in the light of the New Testament interpretation and development of this commandment in the conduct of Jesus himself. Camus points this out impressively in *The Fall,* the novel to which I referred earlier. Müller-Schwefe summarises Camus' account as follows: 'This vicious circle of accusation and defence, condemnation and exposure, was breached once in human history, namely, by Jesus'.[83] Camus refers to the behaviour of Jesus in the episode of the woman accused of adultery. Instead of sharing the indignation of the woman's

accusers, Jesus remains silent. It is a striking fact that the silence of Jesus is mentioned at two important points in the New Testament: once in the Johannine pericope just mentioned (Jn.8:1-11) and again in the passion narrative (Mk.14:55-64). Confronted here with his own accusers – more specifically still, with the false witnesses – 'he was calm and silent and answered nothing'.

The impressively eloquent silence of Jesus in these two specific 'trial situations' prompts reflection. Jesus seems to practise 'passive resistance'. He does not join in the 'outcry' of the 'false witnesses'; he does not accelerate the inexorable movement of the mills of 'justice' which grind mercilessly on and crush so many. His immediate action is to halt them. In no way does he ignore or trivialize the woman's guilt but he judges it graciously and sets her on her feet. In the second case, he submits himself to the judicial mills of church and state, takes his place within the vicious circle of judgement and condemnation and breaks it open. According to the witness of the New Testament, he does this with the eschatological and therefore ultimate right on his side. Henceforward, on the basis of this 'passive resistance', this 'passion', of Jesus, the mills of mercilessness are brought to a standstill; a breach has been made once and for all in the 'logic and consistency' of our eternal prosecuting and judging. Grace has the final word.

Christian faith must show itself to be Christian faith by this advocacy of grace with all its ethical (and political) consequences. In their own 'trial situations', Christians live by the grace which intervenes to liberate and acquit them, and in this way they taste their freedom, just as Paul in his message of justification (in spite of all accusations, justified and unjustified), mastered by grace and conquering by grace, finds ever new ways of formulating this truth and this freedom, borrowing his analogies, significantly, from precisely the language of the lawcourts: 'So then there is now no condemnation for those who are in Christ Jesus . . . Who shall lay a charge against God's elect? . . . It is Christ Jesus who died and, more than that, who was also raised from the dead, who is at the right hand of God, and also intercedes for us'. (Rom.8:1, 33f.) This advocacy of Jesus Christ on our behalf sets us free to become actively and passively advocates of grace, advocates on behalf of our neighbours. We are called, therefore, to refuse to adopt (whether thoughtlessly or with positive zeal) the merciless patterns of human behaviour, or to reinforce merciless relationships and structures, but rather to introduce into our own patterns of behaviour and relationships the standpoints and creative elements of grace and mercy. Justification *and* justice – this phrase which we emphasised earlier – must be allowed its full weight in this direction, too: we must develop our emphatic concern with justice and its institutions within the horizon of grace and mercy. Neither in their churches nor in their societies are Christians at liberty to hide this light of grace 'under a bushel'. This, too, is part of our response to the commandment: 'You shall not bear false witness against your neighbour'.

What is meant by 'Telling the Truth'?

In the development of our argument so far we have kept closely to the findings of Old Testament scholarship and to the more restricted application of the Ninth Commandment in its original meaning. But even as defined on that basis, the problem field was mapped out fairly broadly. In the concluding stretch of my exposition, however, it is necessary to recall the more general problematic mentioned at the beginning of this chapter in connection with the Czech Reformation: the question of the *truth* and *telling the truth*.

'You shall not bear false witness against your neighbour'. Here again, as we turn to the question of truth, we must bear in mind the precise wording of the Ninth Commandment. The question of false – and true – witness does not arise in a merely abstract or general way, so to speak in a spatial and temporal vacuum, but always in a quite specific context and relationship, that of the neighbour. This is really a decisive emphasis for the biblical view of the truth, as distinct from (though not in contradiction of) the understanding of truth in Greek antiquity, for example. The Greek word for truth, *aletheia,* means truth in the sense of a theoretic insight into the structure of reality. Its purpose is the discovery of the hidden, the unveiling of phenomena, and the conceptual grasp of the true ontological realities. The Hebrew term *emeth,* on the contrary, refers to the trustworthiness, reliability, validity and binding character of a personal behaviour, but above all, in a concentrated form, the demonstration of fidelity between persons.

The original model on which this view of truth is based is God's covenant with his people. As the Bible understands it, truth is a 'covenant concept'. In other words, we are to understand truth concretely *in terms of co-humanity*. It is significant that the same point should be emphasised in the apostolic exhortation of the *Letter to the Ephesians,* which is the New Testament pendant to the Ninth Commandment: 'Therefore, putting away falsehood, let every one speak the truth with his neighbour, for we are members one of another' (Eph.4:25). We note here how that little final phrase reinforces the thrust of the Ninth Commandment. Truth refers, therefore, not only and not primarily to the realm of objectively demonstrable facts, but to human behaviour and to human relationships. Truth is not to be defined, therefore, exclusively in individual terms but always socially as well. When 'I' am asked for truth, for true witness, my 'thou' – my fellow human being and my God – is also present. The question of truth is never a 'private matter'. It concerns my existence in the community; it is a social phenomenon.

What does this imply for the ethical problems envisaged by the Ninth Commandment? Two terms suggest themselves as a provisional answer to this question: it implies that the question of truth is *radicalized* and *made concrete.* By the first of these two terms I mean that when we bear false (or true) witness, it is never just a matter of words, that when we break this commandment it is never merely a matter of sins of the tongue. False witness against the neighbour is always a blow struck against our co-humanity, endangering our community with near and distant neighbours. Understood in this way, a lie does not merely touch the verbal surface of life tangentially but strikes at the very roots of our co-existence in marriage, family, church and society. This is what makes the Ninth Commandment so radical and serious and gives Christian ethics its guiding principle: *principia obstat* ('nip the evil in the bud'). In other words, we must tackle the evil in the small everyday 'white lies' to which we are all more or less prone. It is in this light that my earlier reference to Masaryk and that apparently trivial anecdote from his life acquires its significance. Just because 'false witness' is not merely a matter of words, our words take on a deeper, more than merely superficial significance. Even our ordinary 'idle words' must be seen in the light of the Ninth Commandment.

But this radicalizing of the question of truth must also be understood as its *concretization,* and not in some abstract legalistic sense. We find in the history of the problem of truth and lying strong currents in the direction of scrupulosity and casuistry. We are familiar perhaps with Kant's famous statement to the effect that he was too proud ever to tell an untruth, even if a criminal were to ask him with evil intent where a friend in hiding was to be found. We also know of the endless debates about borderline cases of the 'necessary falsehood', for example, telling a dying person, a criminal or a child the truth etc. There is no cause to minimize the importance of this problem. The intensity of Kant's scrupulosity is impressive and the borderline cases just mentioned concern serious problems of life in society. They must be dealt with in ethics and pastoral care. But what is needed first of all is a fundamental clarification. The Ninth Commandment cannot be satisfactorily dealt with in terms of principles and even casuistry (in the sense of examples worked out in advance) fails here. The truth is always concrete. In other words, it is always to be sought and witnessed to in successive concrete situations, and with reference to the human beings involved. But it is the *truth,* not what is arbitrary or opportune, which is concrete, the truth from the standpoint of the commandment, in the light of Christ. And precisely in this light, that means with loving concern and therefore consideration for the neighbour. From this standpoint, a 'ruthless truthfulness' would be a contradiction in terms and a principle such as *fiat veritas pereat mundus* ('let the truth be told and the world perish') would be diabolical not divine wisdom.

One of the most helpful comments on this theme was made by Dietrich Bonhoeffer in one of his last and unfinished writings, *What is Meant by "Telling the Truth".* In this he says: 'The truthfulness which we owe to God must assume a concrete form in the world. Our speech must be truthful not in principle but concretely . . . Telling the truth, therefore, is something which must be learnt . . . Every utterance or word lives and has its home in some particular environment. The word in the family is different from the word in business or in public. The word which has come to life in the warmth of personal relationships is frozen to death in the cold air of public existence'.[84] Bonhoeffer gives an example: 'A teacher asks a child in front of the class whether it is true that his father often comes home drunk. It is true, but the child denies it . . . The child's answer can indeed be called a lie; yet this lie contains more truth . . . than would have been the case had the child betrayed his father's weakness in front of the class . . . The charge of lying recoils on the teacher alone'.[85] In this essay Bonhoeffer dissociates himself above all from any kind of fanaticism about truth. Such fanaticism displays 'nothing but a lifeless image of the truth'. 'He dons the halo of the fanatic devotee of truth who can make no allowance for human weaknesses; but in fact, he is destroying the living truth between human beings.'[86] In his prison papers, Bonhoeffer also emphasises another aspect, one which is very relevant in an age much given to psychologies, even industries, of exposure, in today's 'striptease society'. 'After all, "truthfulness" does not mean uncovering everything that exists. God himself made clothes for human beings (Gen.3:21); and that means that *in statu corruptionis* many things in human life ought to remain covered, and that evil, even though it cannot be eradicated, ought at least to be concealed. Exposure is cynical, and although the cynic prides himself on his exceptional honesty, or claims to want the truth at all costs, he misses the crucial fact . . .'[87]

The theological justification for interpreting the Ninth Commandment in this broader sense as a radicalized and concretized question of truth is to be found in the very centre of the New Testament, in *the event of Christ.* We are told in the Johannine prologue that 'in him the Word became flesh' and that 'grace and truth came through Jesus Christ' (Jn.1:14, 17). I believe this affirmation to be of great importance for our theme. The truth is defined here as the incarnate Word and not, therefore, as mere propositional truth, and it is also linked inseparably with grace. It is in this light that Christians are to see the Ninth Commandment. In the New Testament history of Christ, the question of truth is radicalized and made concrete in a quite specific sense, as a 'symbiosis' of truth and grace. We, too, must strive for the same 'symbiosis' in our understanding and practice of the Ninth Commandment. Or, in free adaptation of a twofold statement which appears in a variety of forms in Blaise Pascal: It is a false love which scorns the truth. But again, it is a false zeal for truth which destroys love. Truthfulness only occurs in the atmosphere of love. We are to bear our witness to the neighbour, by looking towards the witness of Jesus Christ himself, who is also called in the New Testament, *expressis verbis,* 'the true and faithful witness' (Rev.3:14).

The Tenth Commandment:
You Shall Not Covet

Difficulties of Interpretation

The final commandment of the Decalogue seems to present the commentators with more difficulties than the preceding ones, in respect of both form and content. *Formally,* there is the question of the numbering of the commandments. In the Catholic and Lutheran traditions (in contrast to the Orthodox and the Reformed), Exodus 20:17 is counted as two commandments. The beginning of the verse, 'You shall not covet your neighbour's house', is reckoned as the ninth commandment, and the following words, 'You shall not covet your neighbour's wife, nor his manservant, nor his maidservant, nor his ox, nor his ass, nor anything that is your neighbour's', as the tenth. The point of this division, of course, was to arrive at a total of ten commandments, since the prohibition of images (Ex.20:4-6) had been abandoned as a separate commandment and counted with the first. It is almost universally recognized today that this is an artificial solution and that the whole verse 17 is a close-knit unity.

So far as *content* is concerned, an even greater difficulty arises in the light of recent Old Testament scholarship. What exactly is this concluding verse of the whole Decalogue getting at? What is its specific emphasis? In the context of the whole Decalogue, what does it add that is really new? These are relatively new questions. Over most of the history of exegesis, it was considered fairly obvious where the difference between this commandment and the rest was to be located: namely, in the human heart, in the subjective presupposition for all the evil deeds prohibited in the preceding commandments. It was assumed that the law, up to this point focussed on the destructive behaviour of humanity, especially in the Second Table, now needed to concentrate more particularly in conclusion on the driving forces and motives of the human heart.

But it was then pointed out by Old Testament scholars (J. Herrmann was the first to do so in 1927 in a Festschrift for the Old Testament scholar Sellin) that it was hardly natural to take the Hebrew word *chamad* as applying to the 'inner life' of human beings; that on the contrary it points to the violent intrigues by which people seek unlawfully to expropriate other people's property. But this posed the difficult problem of differentiating between the Tenth and Eighth Commandments. Even when it was recognized that the specific sin envisaged in the Eighth Commandment was kidnapping, the boundaries between the two commandments still seem so vague that the Tenth Commandment lost its clear profile. Some scholars solve the problem by taking the Eighth and Tenth Commandments together.[88]

I would not wish to adopt such a drastic solution. Not only because other Old Testament scholars find exegetical grounds for the traditional interpretation,[89] but above all because I find no convincing grounds for discovering dilemmas here anymore than I did in the case of the Eighth Commandment. The reminder that *chamad* not only means 'covetousness' as a disposition of the human will but also includes the actual intrigues leading to the successful expropriation of the coveted object is, to my mind, extremely important.[90] It is a safeguard against all false subjectivity, in the sense of a dualistic distinction between 'soul' and 'world'. This is an important emphasis in Old Testament anthropology. Expressed in contemporary terms, 'theory' and 'praxis' are dialectically interrelated and cannot be divorced from each other. In different contexts, however, the emphasis can and should be placed at different points, since our human life has its – mutually inseparable – 'inward' and 'outward' aspects. It is altogether legitimate and indeed realistic in the interests of liberation to investigate also the subjective factors in 'covetousness'. In basic agreement with traditional exegesis, therefore, but without its idealistic contraction, I find here the specific thrust, the new element, of the Tenth Commandment.

For rounding off the ethical content of the Decalogue, two themes in the Tenth Commandment seem to me especially important, indeed, indispensable. Our attention is drawn to them by the undoubtedly significant repetition of the two basic concepts in Ex.20:17: the term *'covet'* and the term *'neighbour'*, the former occurring twice and the latter three times in this commandment. We shall look at each in turn.

The Sidelong Glance

In this Tenth Commandment more than in any of the others, we are conscious of the social and cultural background: the agrarian patriarchal society of Israel in which wives, slaves and oxen alike are counted as part of a man's property. At first sight this removes the Tenth Commandment in its original form to a distant culture and society quite alien from our own. We find the inclusion of wives in these property relationships particularly rebarbative, of course. We must be careful, however, not to bridge this gap artificially 'by one or two modernizations'; for example, 'by substituting a tractor for the ox, a landrover for the ass, transforming the agricultural cottage into a highrise apartment, the maidservant into a washing machine and the dependent housewife into a professional woman who, like her husband, is away from home all day'.[91] We are quite right to look for concreteness, of course, and this is surely the positive significance of the 'homely' illustrations of 'anything that is your neighbour's. What we said about the truth being concrete, when we were considering the Ninth Commandment, is also true here. But the real topicality and relevance of the Tenth Commandment lies at a deeper level: not in the question of the changing and interchangeable *objects* of our covetousness, but in the actual *dynamics* of this covetousness itself.

But what precisely do we mean by *covetousness?* We should not be too quick to look in one direction only here; that of sexual desire. This was in fact what happened at a very early stage, especially after the Hebrew word had been rendered in the Septuagint by the Greek *ouk epithymeseis*. In the Greek culture it was all too easy to equate *epithymia* with physical desire, i.e. the especially unruly steed of Plato's famous pair. To avoid any misunderstanding, let it be said right away that this area of sexual desire also falls within the scope of the Tenth Commandment. The commandment specifically mentions the

'neighbour's wife'; she is to be protected against attempted
seduction. But the biblical anthropology does not allow us to
develop a lopsided psychology and to play off the 'bright' and
'dark' psychic components against each other. The focal point
of the Tenth Commandment is not sexual desire as such but the
'covetousness' which actually assumes a wide diversity of forms
and covers a broad range of human experiences, including that
of sexuality. In biblical terms, the focal point here is not human
sensuality and sexuality but the human 'heart', i.e. what the
Bible regards as the core and centre of our humanity and all its
impulses.

The whole thrust of the Tenth Commandment in this comprehensive area is summed up in that frank, direct and severe
saying of Jesus: 'For out of the heart come evil thoughts,
murder, adultery, fornication, theft, false witness, slander'
(Mt.15:19). This saying of Jesus contains references to almost
the entire Decalogue. The focal point of this last of the
commandments is the source from which the destruction of
co-human relationships and all breaches of the commandments
of the Decalogue proceed. Therefore: 'You shall not covet'.

We need to be warned here against another enticing over-
simplification. The Tenth Commandment is certainly not prohibiting all impulses, longings, desires and passions. The biblical anthropology does not discriminate against the instinctive
and emotional levels of the human soul. It does not promote an
asceticism in which hunger for life is eliminated as completely
as possible, as in certain radical currents in Buddhism and
other oriental religions. Nor does it recommend in principle the
avoidance of the 'extreme impulses' of our souls and the choice
of the 'golden mean' in every situation, as did certain ethical
movements in classical antiquity. The Old Testament is
peopled with human beings of markedly strong passions who
are not censured on this account. Nor do the notoriously
'lukewarm' have a particularly good press even in the New
Testament (cf.Rev.3:16). It is clear, then, that the Tenth
Commandment is not prohibiting all strong impulses of feeling
or instinct, still less the instinctive level of life as such. On the
contrary, it is a clear warning against desires of a certain kind,
against a selfish encroachment on God and the neighbour.

This brings into view the basic feature, the inner presupposition of what the Bible calls *sin*. In modern cultural history and in the present climate of opinion, the term 'sin' has a suspect flavour, even among theologians. There is a suspicion that it is a bulwark of a pessimistic anthropology and of a capitulating social strategy which hampers all progress. This is a misunderstanding, one for which the practice of the Church must certainly take its share of the blame, of course. From the biblical standpoint, the term 'sin' is a realistic one in view of the world as it is. The specific concrete focus of the Tenth Commandment is the *'sidelong glance'* – the envious comparison we make between ourselves and others, the suspicion that the other person is preferred, privileged, has an unfair advantage. And then the response to this: covetousness finding expression in an effort to catapult ourselves into the other person's position, to make ourselves equal or even more successful, to establish our own 'ego' on some – on *the* – more exalted throne.

Right at the very beginning of the Bible we are given a very accurate and vivid picture of the origins. Take Genesis 3, for example, where the serpent's strategy for dealing with God is presented as the false promise of *hybris:* 'You will be as gods'. Adam falls for this: he does not want to be or remain 'merely' human but to make himself absolute; he does not want 'merely' to tend and cultivate the garden but also to storm the heavens. At every step of the way, therefore, in small things as in great, human history is burdened with this drive towards self-absolutization, which is destructive of others, destructive of itself. Or take Genesis 4, the story of Cain and Abel. Here it is Cain's sidelong glance, his envy of his brother Abel, and then the rapid degeneration of brotherly co-existence into rivalry and conflict, hatred and murder. This, too, is a paradigm depicting in advance the future pattern of human history in all its countless variations, its history of class struggles, race conflicts and greedy rivalry for power and possession.

The Bible and, quite explicitly, the Tenth Commandment warn us against this 'covetousness', this latent tendency of the human heart. Covetousness is seen as the source of alienation in the human world. For it fails to fulfil the fundamental condition of human existence in either of its aspects: the covenant of freedom both before God *and* before the neighbour. The urge to self-divinization certainly seems to offer an anticipation of 'complete' freedom. The attempt to push the brother to one side and even to eliminate him altogether is seen as the enhancement of one's own chances of freedom. But, on both counts, it is an illusory freedom, self-destructive as well as destructive of others. For God's human creatures, to depart from the covenant, to choose the way of ruthlessness, inevitably leads not to liberation but only to a different and even worse 'house of bondage'. Our idols – those inside us as well as those outside us – enslave us.

Biblical anthropology is also realistic in its refusal to moralise even here; when it uses this term 'covet' or 'desire' it has in view not just the obviously 'evil' but also and above all the 'good'. In other words, it is aware of the omnipresence of sin in our human life. Two extremely vivid Old Testament stories will serve to illustrate this aspect of the Tenth Commandment. First, the story of Naboth's vineyard (1 Kings 21). An 'ordinary man' has a vineyard which his king finds very desirable. It would be just the thing to complete the king's estate. But Naboth refuses to part with his ancestral inheritance. His refusal whets the king's appetite for this tiny patch of ground. So much so that he devises a cunning plan to eliminate Naboth and puts it into operation, so obtaining the vineyard over Naboth's dead body. The second story of royal covetousness is found in 1 Samuel 11. This time, the coveted 'object' is not a piece of land but the neighbour's wife, Bathsheba, the wife of Uriah the Hittite, whom the king desires for himself. Once again a cunning plan is devised and once again the human being standing in the king's path is done to death.

There is food for thought in these two stories, their similarities and their differences. The common feature is the behaviour of the two kings; it is these powerful rulers of society who are provoked and seduced into committing brutal acts; obviously starting with their 'sidelong glance' at their neighbours, in spite of the fact that the resources of these neighbours are incomparably more modest. This is an unmistakable aspect of the 'desire syndrome' down to our own day. It is the rich and the powerful in particular – i.e. those who are really in need of nothing – who are weak and vulnerable. In the present context, however, it is the differences which we wish to stress. Although I did not name the two kings in question, we all know who they were. In the first example, it was King Ahab (and Jezebel); in the second, it was King David. What a contrast. Ahab is a classic example of the wicked and bungling dictator; David the king of promise. Two sharply contrasting types, therefore. Yet in the hour of temptation they *both* fail, in relation to both God and the neighbour. Luther was right, therefore, to stress this point in his exposition of the Tenth Commandment: 'This last commandment, therefore, is given not for rogues in the eyes of the world but precisely for the most pious who wish to be praised and to be called honest and upright people, since they have not offended against the former commandments'.[92]

It is now clearest to us, perhaps, that the Tenth Commandment is no mere 'appendix' to the Decalogue, not simply a coda, a redundant 're-take' or 'recap' of what has already been said. It is an incisive radicalizing of the whole perspective. It uncovers the *invisible mass* of the iceberg of sin; it seeks to illuminate the 'dark cellars' of our houses of bondage, to unmask the hidden impulses and mechanisms of our lust for possession and power. It is a summons to us to look into our own hearts and inner inclinations, not just at the world around us and the visible evidence of wickedness and endangered freedom which we see there. And it summons us to conduct this examination in a very concrete and specific way. *Principiis obsta!* Nip the evil in the bud! Root out every ruthless, godless and inhuman desire! It is here, too, that the issue between enslavement and liberation is decided.

But not only here. We cannot restrict our ethical responsibility to this inner realm. With all the previous nine commandments in mind and in view of the comprehensive scope of the Hebrew word *chamad,* no theological interpretation of the Tenth Commandment can possibly forget this. We cannot ignore the *visible effects* of sinful desire, the actual behaviour patterns and social conditions produced by the ensuing alienation, the historical and social sediments deposited by covetousness. Nor can the *systematized covetousness of society* be left out of account here. This is presented clearly and trenchantly by Karl Marx who wrote – a little drastically and with some exaggeration perhaps but, alas, still too close to the truth for comfort – of certain trends in capitalist society: 'No eunuch flatters his despot more basely or uses more infamous means to revive his flagging capacity for pleasure, in order to win a surreptitious favour for himself, than does the eunuch of industry, the manufacturer, in order to sneak himself a silver penny or two or coax the gold from the pocket of his dearly beloved neighbour. Every product is a bait with which to entice the essence of the other, his money. Every real or potential need is a weakness which will tempt the fly on to the lime-twig'.[93]

These tendencies, too, must be examined ethically and politically in the light of the direction pointed by the Tenth Commandment. But here again, the traditional thrust of this commandment must be respected and even fundamentally inescapable extensions must not be permitted to blunt the edge of its direct personal summons. (Moreover, human envy and covetousness do not respect the boundaries between the different systems, as experiences in the countries of 'real socialism' vividly illustrate.) What need to be tackled are the inner sources of our sin, its *dimension of depth*. This is the justification for the unmistakable emphasis of this final commandment: 'You shall not covet'. Hence the prayer of the psalmist (David) with its positive emphasis: 'Create in me a clean heart, O God!' (Ps.51:12). Hence, too, the exhortation of the prophets and apostles to each one of us personally to 'fight the good fight of faith' (1 Tim.6:12). You must fight precisely at the point where you yourself are tempted and assailed by your own specific lust for possession and power. Here is where we are to prove our freedom, cherishing no illusions about our own hearts, yet at the same time indulging in no cynical or weary defeatism. For in the perspective of the whole Decalogue, and we need to recall this here at its end, the summons of the Tenth Commandment is not naked pressure and compulsion, but rather encouragement to us to claim for ourselves the promise with which the Decalogue began: 'I am the Lord your God, who brought you out of the land of Egypt, out of the house of bondage'. The promise of deliverance holds good also, and for faith especially, for the house of bondage of our assailed and covetous hearts. Despite our constant failures and defeats, we are no longer slaves, not even slaves of our own covetousness.

Who is my neighbour?

We turn now to the other main emphasis of the Tenth Commandment: the *neighbour*. This is not the first occurrence of this term in the Decalogue. In the preceding commandment prohibiting false witness, the neighbour is already named as the unmistakable point of reference to whom our witness is addressed. It is in the presence of the neighbour that the truth as an event takes place. But now, at the very end of the Decalogue, in this Tenth Commandment, the term 'neighbour' occurs three times. The covetousness of sinful humanity clearly has this special characteristic: our lust for possession and power not only orbits egotistically around our own personal interests but in doing so also runs counter to the interests of our fellow human beings. It has a social, or rather an antisocial, dynamic destructive of our neighbour's freedom and development, his property, his means of livelihood, his marriage and his private life. The sidelong glance is no vague scanning of the horizon but is fixed on the other, the neighbour. But *who is my neighbour?*

We have every cause to be suspicious of this question. It has a familiar ring. It was asked in an important episode in the New Testament. An expert in the law, confronted by Jesus with the twofold command of love – 'You shall love the Lord your God with all your heart, and with all your soul, and with all your strength, and with all your mind, and your neighbour as yourself' – replied by asking 'And who is my neighbour?' According to Lk.10:25-37, he was trying to justify himself, adopting a strategy only too frequently deployed in ethical contexts, namely, the attempt to evade a clear and binding directive by retreating into general reflections on the 'prolegomena to ethics'. But Jesus meets this strategy in a way which bars the way to such an evasion. He tells the story of the merciful Samaritan, a vivid and compelling answer. But the very form of Jesus' answer underlines the fact that the problem is no general theoretical problem but a concrete and practical one. Indeed, more radically still, the problem (Jesus tells the expert in the law) is not the neighbour but *you yourself*. (It is no accident that in the parable the question takes on a different form to that of the original question and is also given a pointedly personal application: 'Which of these three, do *you* think, proved neighbour *to* the man who fell among the robbers?' Indirectly, of course, the 'general question' also receives an answer here: the 'neighbour' is the human being you encounter on your way, the person who is your contemporary, the person who shares your space and time. Just as the truth is concrete, so also is the neighbour.

In approach at least, this corresponds to the use of the term 'neighbour' in the Decalogue: the Hebrew word *'rea'* means 'the fellow human being, the neighbour, the person one encounters, without any precise legal definition'.[94] Over long stretches of the Old Testament history, of course, the commandment was taken to refer to the covenant partners within the people of God, but the scope of its application nevertheless remained indefinite, particularly within the eschatological horizon. This is where Jesus picks up the threads, both in his vivid summons to concreteness, to love of the neighbour as we have seen clearly in the parable of Lk.10 and also in his challenging reference to the Samaritans in the same parable. The concept of neighbour cannot be tied down to natural conditions and characteristics and then restricted to these.

This dialectic in the concept of the 'neighbour' appears also in the ethical teaching of the apostles, sometimes with reference to the example of Jesus. 'So then, as we have opportunity, let us do good to all, and especially to those who are of the household of faith' (Gal.6:10). This Pauline formula guards against a twofold danger. On the one hand there is the temptation to an indefinite abstract love which remains so general and widesweeping that it simply ignores the 'nearest neighbour'. This is the constant temptation of idealistic internationalists and political theologians. But on the other hand, there is the danger of a provincial and selectively restricted solidarity which applies exclusively to one's own 'kith and kin' and which cultivates and develops only their 'islands of the blest' without any heed to the need and distress out there in the world. This is the temptation of parochial and sectarian pietists and pragmatists. The former are called to order by Paul's words: *'especially* to those who are of the household of faith', which insist on concreteness, while the latter are called to order by the injunction to 'do good to *all'* which removes all restrictions. It is in this dialectic of obligatory concreteness and dynamic openness that the question of the 'neighbour' is posed and answered whenever obedience to the Tenth Commandment is required.

John Calvin summed up the position admirably in his *Institutes.* At the end of his exposition of the Decalogue, he answers the question 'Who is my neighbour?' as follows: 'The more closely human beings are bound together by the ties of kinship, of acquaintanceship, or of neighbourhood, the more responsibilities for one another they share ... But I say: we ought to embrace the whole human race without exception in a single feeling of love ... whatever the character of the human being, we must love him or her because we love God'.[95] In this sense, too, we are to heed the warning that God and humanity – the two Tables of the Decalogue – are inseparable.

There is a further point in the words of Paul just quoted which can help us in our interpretation of the Tenth Commandment. Paul speaks of 'opportunity', of the *kairos,* of the summons of the time given us by God. As I have stressed more than once, the Decalogue is not a 'timeless' document and the commandments are not rigid rules and regulations. We are provided here with a signpost to freedom, on the basis of the Exodus, a signpost which we are each to respect and follow in our own day and age. It points the way to no arbitrary freedom but to a freedom which is only to be found in the direction indicated by the commandments. But we have always to recognize and respond to the 'signs of the times', to the *kairos,* to the 'opportunity'. This also applies to the question of the neighbour and to love of the neighbour today.

This being the case, it seems to me to be high time and most important that we Christians in affluent societies should in particular grasp and accept the radical implications of Jesus' concept of the neighbour in our time and place. The concrete neighbour on our own doorstep (and in our own homes, in our dealings with our 'nearest neighbours') must still be emphasised, of course. Even in the midst of our material affluence there is still much distress and lack of neighbourly love – not to mention a good deal of destructive covetousness – and we must not be blind to this. 'Home missions' and Christian service agencies are by no means redundant in our prosperous societies. But, in our global ecumenical situation today, it becomes more urgent than ever to emphasise the other aspect, the need to *broaden our horizons of solidarity,* far beyond national and continental boundaries, so as to include our 'distant neighbours', especially those in the most desperately threatened countries of the so-called 'Third World'. Human beings and nations are becoming mutually interdependent on a global scale for the first time in the history of our planet. In consequence we are becoming each other's neighbours in the biblical sense in a correspondingly global sense, people in encounter and in contact, and dependent on one another. In these circumstances, therefore, drastic disparities in living conditions become in the end intolerable. If we fail to reduce and bridge the gap between first and third class passengers on this 'spaceship Earth' by mutual solidarity, the prospects for the future are gloomy indeed, and this in all three 'worlds'. As was rightly stressed at the Nairobi Assembly of the World Council of Churches (and on many other occasions besides), our 'Titanic is on collision course'.

It is, above all, the rich *western churches* who are confronted with a special challenge here, and this indeed in the context of the Tenth Commandment. For how often in our relationships with our fellow human beings have we 'western peoples' displayed the characteristics of a peculiarly covetous type of human being. How often from our position of power have we coveted our neighbour's house, our neighbour's wife, our neighbour's property and 'anything that is our neighbour's'! Not just within our own civilization but also abroad throughout the earth. The colonial era is a sobering illustration of the truth of this. The Tenth Commandment is a sword thrust right to the heart and to the history of the West, therefore. Not that the commandment is meant to lead us to indulge in masochistic self-laceration or to cripple us with guilt complexes. It is a summons, rather, to repentance and liberation. We are called to acknowledge our deeply ingrained lust for possession and power in private life, in national life, and in the world of nations, to see them for what this lust really is, nothing other than a 'house of bondage' (despite the 'fleshpots of Egypt' we have enjoyed and still enjoy inside it). We are called, therefore, to venture out in an 'Exodus' towards a more just life of solidarity, and here too, in our private life, in national life and in international life. This is not an easy thing for any of us to do. The inner and outer pressures of our covetousness militate against our doing it. But if we wish to survive, this fresh start is absolutely essential and must be ventured, even if only small minorities can be persuaded of its necessity and begin to move.

Should it not be the 'people of God' above all which should prove itself to be 'the forward troops of life' (Gollwitzer) already moving in this direction? For the heirs of the Old Testament and the New are not just constrained by historical necessity to create more just conditions for common human survival, as the rest of humankind is, but also at the same time by the 'signpost to freedom' which strengthens and upholds them even in times of individual and collective folly. The Decalogue, its final commandment – and the radical version of this commandment in the Sermon on the Mount and in the practice of Jesus – take on a new freshness and contemporaneity for us. My Prague friend and teacher, Josef B. Soucek, was fond of pointing out in the sixties the astonishing convergence between the most urgent challenges of our time and the radical message of Jesus, a message which has so often been branded as 'fanatical' by theologians, and therefore as offering no real guidance in the field of social ethics and politics. 'It can confidently be stated that human life cannot continue much longer unless in critical moments leading statesmen are ready to accept insights which in the last analysis stem from the Sermon on the Mount. This should both humble the churches and also encourage them to present their message with greater boldness and firmness.' [96]

I can only endorse this view. The central task for Christian theology and ethics continues to be to ensure that the 'salt of Jesus' – and the salt of the Ten Commandments – does not lose its savour because of any lukewarmness on our part but continue to bring its guiding and lifegiving power to bear on the tumultuous times in which we live.

An Eccentric Ethic

With these reflections on the biblical view of the neighbour, we reach the end of our exposition of the Decalogue. We do well to bear in mind the dynamic movement we have traced here.

We began with the concept of the divine Name, the concept which controls all the rest. Then we came to the fellow human being. This is the direction and movement of a Christian ethic: from God to the neighbour. An 'eccentric' ethic? Yes, in a quite specific sense. Yet this 'eccentricity' entails no loss of our own identity. On the contrary, what happens is the real history of our individual and social life, the struggle for a freedom which does not revolve around itself but which seeks and finds the fulness of personal life *coram Deo et proximo* ('in the presence of God and the neighbour'). 'For whoever would save his or her life, will lose it; and whoever loses his or her life for my sake and the Gospel's will save it' (Mk.8:35). The Decalogue points us the way.

NOTES

Introduction

1. Gerhard Ebeling, *Die Zehn Gebote,* J. C. B. Mohr (Paul Siebeck), Tübingen 1973, p. 15.
2. *op. cit.* p. 21.
3. As cited by Ebeling, *op. cit.* p. 30.
4. Gerhard von Rad, *Theology of the Old Testament,* SCM Press Ltd., London 1975 Vol. I p. 193.
5. *op. cit.* p. 193.
6. *ibid.*

Preamble

7. Karl Marx, *Early Writings,* Pelican Marx Library, p. 356.
8. Ernst Bloch, *Atheismus im Christentum,* p. 22. (The passage is omitted in the published English translation.)

The First Commandment

9. *Concordia,* or *Book of Concord, The Symbols of the Evangelical Lutheran Church,* St. Louis Mo., Concordia Publishing House 1957, p. 159ff.
10. Cf. W. F. Albright, *From the Stone Age to Christianity, Monotheism and the Historical Process,* Baltimore, John Hopkins Press, 1940.
11. *op. cit.* Vol. I p. 210f. Cf. J. J. Stamm, *Der Dekalog im Lichte der neueren Forschung,* 2nd ed. Berne 1962, p. 54. Cf. the French translation by Ph. Reymond, *Le Decalogue à la lumière des recherches contemporaines,* Delachaux et Niestlé 1959, p. 50 f.
12. *Die Religion in Geschichte und Gegenwart,* 3rd ed. Vol. II, p. 1689.
13. *The School of Faith, The Catechisms of the Reformed Church,* tr. and ed. Thomas F. Torrance, James Clarke & Co. Ltd. London 1959, p. 5.

The Second and Third Commandments

14. von Rad, *Theology of the Old Testament,* Vol. I p. 213.
15. *ibid.* p. 218.
16. Brecht, *Gesammelte Werke* 12, *Werkausgabe,* p. 386.
17. Max Frisch, *Tagebuch 1946-1949,* p. 32 f.
18. *ibid.* p. 30 f.
19. Ebeling, *op. cit.* p. 49.
20. *ibid.* p. 63.
21. von Rad, *op. cit.* Vol. I p. 184.
22. H. R. Müller-Schwefe, *Die Zehn Gebote,* p. 31.
23. von Rad, *op. cit.* Vol I p. 183.
24. L. Ragaz, *Die Revolution der Bibel,* p. 11.
25. *ibid.*
26. H. G. Fritzche, *Evangelische Ethik. Die Gebote Gottes als Grundprinzipien christlichen Handelns,* Berlin, Ev. Verlagsanstalt, 1961. p. 57.

The Fourth Commandment
27. Karl Barth, *Church Dogmatics,* Vol. III, Part 4, T & T Clark, Edinburgh 1961, p. 213 (slightly reworded).
28. T. Zahn, *Skizzen aus dem Leben der Alten Kirche,* Zürich 1956, p. 161.
29. Cf. E. Jenni, *Die theologische Begründung des Sabbatgebotes im AT,* Zollikon-Zürich, Ev. Verlag 1956, Theol. Studien No. 46, p. 10 f.
30. Jenni, *op. cit.* p. 7.
31. Jenni, *op. cit.* p. 15.
32. Jenni, *op. cit.* p. 25.
33. Jenni, *op. cit.* p. 26.
34. Fritzsche, *op. cit.* p. 81.
35. Ebeling, *op. cit.* p. 97.
36. *ibid.*
37. Fritzsche cites this from Hagenbach, *Kirchengeschichte,* Vol. 5, 1871, p. 222.
38. Fritzsche, *op. cit.* p. 89.

The Fifth Commandment
39. Ebeling, *op. cit.* p. 115 f.
40. *ibid.* p. 105.

The Sixth Commandment
41. Bo Reicke, *Die Zehn Worte,* p. 59.
42. Ebeling, *op. cit.* p. 121.
43. J. J. Stamm, *op. cit.* p. 54.
45. Calvin, *Institutes,* II, vii, 39, McNeill and Battles, SCM Press Ltd. Vol. I, p. 404.
46. *Concordia,* p. 181 f.
47. Fritzsche, *op. cit.* p. 126.
48. *Church Dogmatics,* III, 4. p. 405.
49. Fritzsche, *op. cit.* p. 134.
50. In *Reformatio* 1975, p. 134 ff. and 203 ff.
51. *op. cit.* p. 210.
52. *op. cit.* p. 211.
53. Cf. J. M. Lochman, *Perspektiven politischer Theologie,* Zürich, Theologischer Verlag, 1971, *Polis* No. 42. p. 35.

The Seventh Commandment
54. H. J. Kraus, *Reich Gottes: Reich der Freiheit, Grundriss systematischer Theologie,* Neukirchener Verlag 1975, p. 359.
55. *Church Dogmatics,* III/4 p. 117 (slightly reworded).
56. *ibid* III/4 p. 118 (slightly reworded).
57. Karl Marx, *Early Writings,* Pelican Marx Library 1975, p. 347.
58. Paul Althaus, *Grundriss der Ethik,* p. 91.
59. *Church Dogmatics,* III/4 p. 140.
60. *ibid.* p. 133.

61. H. J. Kraus, *op. cit.* p. 360.
62. *ibid.*
63. Dietrich Bonhoeffer, *Ethics,* tr. N.H. Smith, 1955, Fontana Library 1964, p. 281.

The Eighth Commandment

64. H. J. Kraus, *op. cit.* p. 361.
65. J. J. Stamm, *op. cit.* p. 58 f.
66. Claus Westermann, in *Zum Thema Menschenrechte,* ed. Jörg Baur, p. 17 and p. 11.
67. Kraus, *op. cit.* p. 362.
68. *Book of Concord,* p. 184, col. 2.
69. L. Ragaz, *Die Revolution der Bibel,* p. 26.
70. Ebeling, *op. cit.* p. 161.
71. Theses on Feuerbach, in *Early Writings,* Pelican Marx Library, p. 423.
72. W. Lüthi, *Die zehn Gebote Gottes,* p. 191 f.
73. *Early Writings,* p. 251.

The Ninth Commandment

74. W. Lüthi, *op. cit.* p. 206.
75. J. J. Stamm, *op. cit.* p. 61 f.
76. *ibid.*
77. Albert Camus, *The Fall,* tr. Justin O'Brien, Penguin Books 1963, p. 81.
78. W. Lüthi, *op. cit.* p. 206.
79. H. R. Müller Schwefe, *op. cit.* p. 110 f. Cf. Camus, *The Fall,* p. 85.
80. J. J. Stamm, *op. cit.* p. 61.
81. *Book of Concord,* p. 187.
82. *ibid.* p. 188.
83. H. R. Müller Schwefe, *op. cit.* p. 114. Cf. Camus, *The Fall,* p. 85.
84. Dietrich Bonhoeffer, *Ethics,* pp. 364, 367.
85. *ibid.* p. 367.
86. *ibid.*
87. Bonhoeffer, *Letters and Papers from Prison,* enl. ed. Bethge, SCM Press Ltd. London 1971, p. 158.

The Tenth Commandment

88. E.g. J. J. Stamm, H. van Oyen, and others.
89. W. L. Moran, *The Conclusion of the Decalogue,* 1967. Cf. B. S. Childs, *The Book of Exodus,* 1974. p. 425 ff.
90. So J. J. Stamm, *op. cit.* p. 57.
91. Ebeling, *op. cit.* p. 197.
92. *Book of Concord,* p. 189.

93. Marx, *Early Writings,* p. 359. Cf. also J. M. Lochman, *Marx begegnen,* Gütersloher Verlagshaus Gerd Mohn, 1975. (An English translation of this book appeared in 1977 under the title *Encountering Marx.*)

94. J. Kühlewein, in Jenni-Westermann, *Theolog. Handwörterbuch AT,* vol. II, p. 790.

95. *Institutes,* II, viii, 55, McNeill and Battles translation, vol. I. p. 418 f. *Responsible Government in a Revolutionary Age,* edited by Z. K. Matthews, SCM Press, London 1966. p. 111.

Index of Names

Alt, A. 119
Althaus, P. 113
Augustine 65

Barth, K. 31f., 58, 67, 89, 96, 108, 113f.
Bloch, E. 161
Bonhoeffer, D. 28, 118, 144f.
Brecht, B. 50

Calvin, J. 42, 92, 157
Camus, A. 137, 140
Capek, K. 134
Chelcicky, P. 104
Childs, B. S. 163
Clausewitz 103

Dibelius (Bishop) 80

Ebeling, G. 14f., 20, 52, 77, 79, 82, 87

Frisch, M. 50f.
Fritzche, H. G. 55, 67, 69f.

Gollwitzer, H. 123, 159

Heidegger, M. 68
Herrmann, J. 148
Hromadka, J. L. 51
Hus, J. 126, 133f.

Jenni, E. 60, 62

Kafka, F. 137
Kant, I. 29, 144
Kierkegaard, S. 68
King, M. L. 104
Knox, J. 43
Kraus, H. J. 106, 116, 119

Lehmann, P. 32
Lönning (Bishop) 98
Luther, M. 15, 33, 42, 92, 126, 140
Lüthi, W. 127, 129, 138

Marx, K. 22f., 29f., 39, 109, 128, 131, 153f.
Masaryk, Th. G. 10, 134, 143
Moran, W. L. 163
Müller-Schwefe, H. R. 140

Nietzsche, F. 115

van Oyen, H. 32, 163

Palach, J. 95, 134f.
Pascal, B. 146
Patocka, J. 10

von Rad, G. 18, 35, 45ff.
Radl, E. 10
Ragaz, L. 54f., 127
Reicke, B. 87
Röthlisberger, H. 15ff., 20

Saner, H. 98f., 100f.
Schweitzer, A. 79
Solzhenitsyn, A. 124
Soucek, J. B. 159
Spener, Ph. J. 69f.
Stamm, J. J. 161ff.

Tertullian 99

Weber, M. 70
Weizsäcker, C. F. von 103
Westermann, C. 163f.

Zahn, Th. 59

Index of Biblical References

Gen. 1:27   108
      1:28   25
      2:18   108
      3   151
      3:21   145
      4   89f. 151
      4:15   90
      9:6   89
      31:19ff.   40

Ex.   20   60
      20:1-17   11
      20:2   21
      20:4-6   147
      20:11   61
      20:15   119, 125
      20:17   147, 149
      21:14   90
      21:16   120f.
      32   36

Deut. 5:2-4   19
      5:12ff.   60
      15:15   122
      24:7   120f.
      29:10ff.   19
      31:10f.   18

2 Sam. 11   152

1 Ki. 21   152

Ps.   6:5   26
       51:12   154
       119   9, 31

Prov. 6:6-11   69

Hos.   2:16ff.; 20ff.; 3:1ff.   110

Mt.   5:1-12   132
       5:21ff.   88, 91, 131
       5:25   92

       5:27ff.   107
       5:27   131
       5:33   131
       6:19ff.   132
       6:24   38, 130
       6:25ff.   68
       15:19   150
       20:15   129
       22:37   33, 40
       23:24   58

Mk.   2:27   64
       3:31ff.   80
       8:35f.   160
       14:55ff.   136
       14:55-64   141

Lk.   10   156
       10:25-37   155
       12:20   68
       12:13-21   68
       19:11ff.   129

Jn.   1:14, 17   145
       8:1-11   105, 141
       18:37   135

Acts   5:29   80

Rom.   7:24   26
       7:24f.   27
       8:1, 33f.   141
       8:38   27
       12:19   90f.
       12:20f.   91f.

1 Cor. 13:4ff.   118

2 Cor. 4:4-6   52

Gal.   3:28   123
       5:1   34

	5:13	35	1 Tim.	6:10	38
	6:10	156		6:12	154
Eph.	4:25	143	Heb.	4:10	65
	6:1, 4	82			
	6:2	83	Rev.	3:14	146
Col.	1:15	52		3:16	150